sex

www.thegoodwebguide.co.uk

thegoodwebguide

sex

matt & jenny blythe

The Good Web Guide Limited • London

First Published in Great Britain in 2000 by The Good Web Guide Limited
Broadwall House, 21 Broadwall, London, SE1 9PL

www.sex.thegoodwebguide.co.uk

Email:feedback@thegoodwebguide.co.uk

Original series concept by Steve Bailey.

10 9 8 7 6 5 4 3 2 1

A catalogue record for this book is available from the British Library.

ISBN 1-903282-09-8

Project Editors Michelle Clare & Haydn Kirnon

Design by Myriad Creative Ltd.

Additional Design by Zoe Marshall.

Printed in Italy at LEGO S.p.A.

the good web guides

The World Wide Web is a vast resource, with millions of sites on every conceivable subject. There are people who have made it their mission to surf the net: cyber-communities have grown, and people have formed relationships and even married on the net.

However, the reality for most people is that they don't have the time or inclination to surf the net for hours on end. Busy people want to use the internet for quick access to information. You don't have to spend hours on the internet looking for answers to your questions and you don't have to be an accomplished net surfer or cyber wizard to get the most out of the web. It can be a quick and useful resource if you are looking for specific information.

The Good Web Guides have been published with this in mind. To give you a head start in your search, our researchers have looked at hundreds of sites and what you will find in the Good Web Guides is a collection of reviews of the best we've found.

The Good Web Guide recommendation is impartial, and all the sites have been visited several times. Reviews are focused on the website and what it sets out to do, rather than an endorsement of a company, or their product. A small but beautiful site run by a one-man band may be rated higher than an ambitious but flawed site run by a mighty organisation.

Relevance to the UK-based visitor is also given a high premium: tantalising as it is to read about purchases you can make in California, because of delivery charges, import duties, and controls it may not be as useful as a local site.

Our reviewers considered a number of questions when reviewing the sites, such as: How quickly do the sites and individual pages download? Can you move around the site easily and get back to where you started, and do the links work? Is the information up to date and accurate? And is the site pleasing to the eye and easy to read? More importantly, we also asked whether the site has something distinctive to offer, whether it be entertainment, inspiration, or pure information. On the basis of the answers to these questions, sites are given ratings out of five. As we aim only to include sites that we feel are of serious interest, there are very few low-rated sites.

Bear in mind that the collection of reviews you see here is just a snapshot of the sites at a particular time. The process of choosing and writing about sites is a bit like painting the Forth Bridge: as each section appears complete, new sites are launched and others are modified. If you register at the Good Web Guide site you can check out the reviews of new sites and updates of existing ones.

As this is the first edition of the Good Web Guide, all our sites have been reviewed by the author and research team, but we would like to know what you think. Contact us via the website or email feedback@thegoodwebguide.co.uk. You are welcome to recommend sites, quibble about the ratings, point out changes and inaccuracies, or suggest new features to assess.

You can find us at:
www.sex.thegoodwebguide.co.uk

contents

user key

- £ subscription required
- R registration required
- (padlock) secure online ordering
- UK country of origin
- ♀ female orgasm rating
- ♂ male orgasm rating

introduction

Love it or hate it, the internet has provided a level of access to sexual material that would have seemed inconceivable just a few years ago. As both liberals and libertines, we are firmly in favour, just so long as everything on show is between informed, consenting adults. This is the policy we have followed in choosing our reviews, although we can take no responsibility for changes in sites made after our visits, nor for where links may lead. Despite the scare stories, the vast bulk of sex sites are innocuous to all but the most repressed.

The internet contains a staggering number of sex sites, and not surprisingly with such an anarchic system, these include the good, the bad, the ugly, and even the actually criminal. Everything anyone could possibly want is there, or just about anything anyway. Finding it may not be so simple, especially if you have unusual tastes. In writing this guide we have tried to make access to net sex simple, quick, and preferably free. Unfortunately, the net is full of traps for the unwary, so firstly, some basic advice:

- You don't need to pay: there's plenty for free.
- If you do decide to pay, be careful about giving credit card details.
- Only download software if you are confident it is virus free.
- Don't be naïve. Go in with common sense and a little scepticism.

It would be easy to write a book on all the rackets out there designed to part surfers from their money. Good, genuinely free sites are rare, and seldom last long as when they become popular bandwidth charges will scare off all but the most determined host. This is a big problem for general sex sites, less so for specialist ones; if you're into worn-out army boots you're probably okay. Many of the good free sites on the net are now specialist. Most free sites now pay for themselves by hosting banners for paysites, and as the host is paid by each click on the banner, it is considered polite to visit the sponsors, although you don't have to sign up. This system is something of a house of cards, and it may well collapse. Other free gallery sites often prove to be bait to get you into paysites. Despite all this, at present there are enough free pictures and stories available to keep anyone happy for life without ever visiting a paysite. This is less true if you like video.

Banners, Pop-Ups and other advertising material may be irritating or even a severe nuisance, and in this guide we have avoided sites which include an unacceptable level of advertising material. Most banners are simple adverts; others are designed to be misleading. Invitations such as 'Click Here for Free Galleries', or 'Play Young Teen Masturbates Video' are never what they seem. Explosions of pop-ups can also be annoying, with dozens of unwanted adverts in small windows obscuring the screen. Even more irritating are pages that attempt to trap the surfer by disabling the Back function on your browser or even going to a full screen so that the only way out seems to be to join the site. It is always possible to get out of these traps, although they are becoming more common and more elaborate. If the worst comes to the worst, you can always reset your computer. Actually, we have decided that these must be designed by aliens, as nobody with any understanding of human nature at all could possibly think that anybody would actually pay up!

Adult Verification System (AVS) sites are not free, nor do they have very much to do with restricting access to sex sites. Basically you pay for membership of the AVS, which gets you an access ID to all those sites using that particular system. What it doesn't guarantee is that the site is any good. The charges for AVS are obviously far greater than would be needed just for administration, and what actually happens is that the AVS provider gives some of your money to the site from which you joined, so you are effectively paying for site access anyway. Several AVS systems exist, and some allow access to only a handful of sites. The biggest, Adult Check, covers thousands of sites, but many are only available to Adult Check Gold members, which is a great deal more expensive to join. Basically, AVS sites are just designed to part you from your money, so don't bother with it.

Free Trial Memberships and sites that offer access in return for your credit-card details are best avoided. They may be honest, they may not. Why risk it? Downloading software to allow free access is an even bigger risk, laying you open to all sorts of potentially expensive scams. One to be careful of is using long-distance phone lines rather than the internet. This may speed things up, but also means paying long-distance rates, a proportion of which will go to the site you are accessing. In general, be aware that 'Free' is not always what it means. There is no advertising standards system on the net, and many apparent promises will simply be lies.

Paysites are rarely worth bothering about in our opinion. Why pay when you can get it for free? This is particularly true for picture sites, when in most cases you only get the same old pictures recycled again and again, and these are often just scans of magazines or video captures, frequently used without copyright permission. Interactive sites are more often worth paying for, but are still open to all sorts of abuse and can prove very expensive. You may also discover difficulties in cancelling your membership, that you have only paid for partial access to the site, or even that large sums have been debited from your account, the site is closed and the hosts are rumoured to be in Paraguay. Remember, for everyone who genuinely wants to entertain you there are a hundred who just want your money, as much as possible, as fast as possible. If you must join a paysite, make it the site of a big, trustworthy organisation, such as Penthouse (www.penthouse.com) or Playboy (www.playboy.com), or at very least one that comes recommended with a proven track record. Among big, well-established paysites, Kara's Adult Playground (www.karasxxx.com) and Danni's Hard Drive (www.danni.com) are perhaps worth a mention.

And remember, buyer beware.

Surfing

Surfing for sex should be simply a matter of following links until you get what you want. Unfortunately, it is not quite so simple. Even in genuine sites the link you want may be hidden among adverts or fancy design. To avoid problems, always wait until a page is fully loaded before moving on, and check to make sure you are clicking on a link that will take you to where you want to go. If in doubt, run your cursor over a link and information on where it is going to take you will appear in the information bar of your browser. This information will change as the cursor moves between active link areas. For instance, a common scam is to have a banner saying 'Gallery 1 Gallery 2 Gallery 3 Gallery 4', so that it appears to be the jumpstation for the galleries of the site you are in. However, if you run your cursor over the area, you will see that the information on where it will take you does not change, showing it to be a single link, undoubtedly to some huge banner-farm advertising paysites.

At your destination, clicking the right hand button of your mouse on the page will bring up a list of options, including one to bookmark the site. When bookmarking, be sure the information that comes up in the save window is relevant, otherwise you may have trouble finding the site again as your library grows. Right clicking on a picture will allow you to save it to disc, but be sure to allow it to load fully first.

The net being what it is, a lot of time will be spent at US sites, which is fine unless you want to shop or go out. Japan is another major player, and the country where language is most often a problem. Japanese comes out as gibberish on most browsers, as do any other non-Roman-alphabet characters. Most sites are either in English or provide an English alternative. We looked at sites across Europe without difficulty and even managed in Indonesia. China alone defeated us.

Software

For basic porn surfing, any browser will allow you to view and save pictures and stories. If you want to make a gallery of your favourites, we recommend the Polyview image-handling program. You can download this from www.polybytes.com as a free trial, and the full range of features becomes enabled when you buy it. If you feel the need for a bigger choice of more sophisticated graphics software, try www.salemcounty.com which lists and reviews an extensive range.

Viewing video requires software which is less likely to be included in a basic package. Real Player 8 claims to allow you to access over 85 per cent of video and audio files available on the net. This is available from www.real.com as a free download for the basic version.

Interactive net sex generally requires specialist software. Some details are given in the Interactive chapter, but most websites will provide links for any software that needs to be downloaded. Failing that, use a search engine to track down the support site for the software you need.

Section 01

tips and techniques

Sex is the oldest and most fundamental of human fascinations, and this fascination spills over onto the internet. Ironically though, if you are looking for sites to educate and inform you about sex, your search could quite easily grind to a halt. Though there is a seemingly infinite choice of sex sites on the internet, to retrieve anything useful, you have to first get past a dense layer of sites which exist purely to titillate. The same sites also either assume that you already know a great deal about sex, or more likely, just don't care. It would be quite easy to spend months surfing sex sites on the internet, and still not learn anything about sex.

The following sites are some of the best sex-information sites that we have discovered on the web. Their focus is on information, which will help you build a healthy foundation for sexual expression both emotionally and physically. The information they contain is not a set of rules, and there can be many different opinions, expressed within one site. All the sites listed, though, give you some idea of the diversity of sex, and aim to give individuals the confidence to express their sexuality, whatever their orientation or preferences.

www.about.com

About.com

overall rating:
★★★★★
classification:
portal
updated:
regularly
navigation:
★★★
content:
★★★★★
readability:
★★★★★
orgasm rating:
not applicable
orgasm rating:
not applicable
speed:
★★★★
US

About.com is a network of sites led by guides who are experts in their respective fields. You won't find the sex section on the homepage, but it's easy enough to access by entering the word 'sex' in the search facility that appears towards the top of the homepage. The result takes you to a vast and eclectic selection of sites, where the topics range from improving your sex life, through using sex as a marketing tool, to straightforward porn.

The results of the search are displayed as a list of hyperlinks. You can move through the list by clicking on the red chevrons at the bottom of the section. Once you're through to a linked site, the About.com warning page will appear. This can be confusing if you are checking out several links, and gives you the feeling of going round in circles, though it's not unworkable.

With over 13,000 linked sites, there is bound to be some overlap with other portals. However, the information sites produced by About.com put the network into a league of its own, and if what you want is straightforward information on sex, and don't have a clue where to look, this would be a good place to start.

SPECIAL FEATURES

Sex 101 – Step by Step Tips and Techniques is an A to Z of sex, with hundreds of listed topics. It is fairly 'vanilla' in attitude, with plenty of tutorials on improving the fundamentals of sex, such as masturbation and giving good oral sex, but there are useful pointers for people who want to venture into something more exotic. There is a useful section on Adult Internet Surfing, which gives step-by-step instructions on disputing credit-card bills if you've been overcharged, killing annoying pop-up windows and signing up safely for a free trial.

Sexuality Site This site is run by a licensed sexologist and is another useful and vast resource if you want to learn more about your own sexuality. The style is friendly and unpatronising, and there is straightforward and clear information about sexual dysfunction, sexuality and disability, STDs and contraception.

Sex is not a dirty word is an invaluable section on sexuality for those with physical or intellectual disabilities. It covers such topics as coping with sexual desires and needs, expressing those needs to a partner, meeting a partner, and techniques for enriching sex, mentally and physically. There is also a substantial archive of support resources, from books to contacts.

If you are a novice at adult surfing, and want plain and simple information on any aspect of sexuality, this is the best place to start.

http://www.beaumontsociety.org.uk

The Beaumont Society

This is the site for the Beaumont Society, Britain's oldest transvestite support group, founded in 1966. Their experience shows, and the site provides a pretty comprehensive resource for their speciality, although the emphasis is firmly on support and advice for men who wish to dress as women, and the site would be less useful for other cross-dressing groups. The presentation is clear and the style relaxed if perhaps a little defensive. The site is adequately fast, very readable, and easy to follow, especially with so much information presented.

overall rating:
★★★★★
classification:
service
updated:
occasionally
navigation:
★★★★
content:
★★★★★
readability:
★★★★★
orgasm rating:
not applicable
orgasm rating:
not applicable
speed:
★★★
UK

SPECIAL FEATURES

With 27 categorised sub-sections we were a little daunted, but each one speaks for itself. They are: About Us, Contact Info, Magazine, Event Diary, Regular Meetings, Late News, President's Page, WOBS (for women in relationships with transvestites), Partner's Help, Join Us, C D Beaumont, Society History, Problem Page, Talks and Visits, seven categories of Links, Gallery, e Beaumont, Guest Book, Search Site, Glossary, and email Us. Click on each and the full list is still present, making for efficient navigation.

We looked at About Us, which discusses the society, its history and aims. CD Beaumont gives the history of the remarkable 18th century transvestite after whom the society is named. The Problem Page covers the commonest problems for transvestites in Question and Answer format. There were only five of these, but they welcome other questions. Links 1 lists 17 individual transvestite homepages, although without details of what each contains. Links 4 is Out and About, a listing of 17 links to clubs and societies for transvestites. Links 5 is TV Suppliers and Services, covering links to 47 online stores for clothing of all types, shoes and wigs, bookstores, and makeover parlours.

OTHER FEATURES

In addition to the above, links are offered to the TG Girls, Global Transgender, and CrossDressWebrings.

An ideal start point and essential resource for all transvestite issues.

www.minou.com/aboutsex

About Sex

overall rating:
★★★★
classification:
information
updated:
regularly
navigation:
★★★★
content:
★★★★
readability:
★★★★
orgasm rating:
not applicable
orgasm rating:
not applicable
speed:
★★★★★
US

About sex is devoted to providing information leading to safe and consensual forms of sexual expression. The content is provided by well-informed amateurs and as such has a down-to-earth and empathic feel that you wouldn't necessarily get from an expert, despite their knowledge. Inevitably, this can lead to a certain amateurishness, with gaps in some areas of the site. However, the extent and quality of the content generally makes up for this. The language is forthright, and the site is suitable for those who are about to start an active sex life, or those who have recently started having sex. Topics range from doing it for the first time to anal sex. Strangely, for a site aimed at the virgin/recent ex-virgin, the banner ads are fairly hardcore. As well as being potentially off-putting to the intended readership, in some sections they are at best inappropriate and at worst offensive.

The homepage consists of a simple list of topics, accompanied by a simple synopsis. To access, simply click on the topic name.

SPECIAL FEATURES

The First Time is a comprehensive his-and-hers guide to losing your virginity, including where you should do it and when you should do it. They're careful to say that it's not a list of rules but a set of guides to ensure that losing your virginity is special, and makes you feel good, which extends to not worrying about the risk of pregnancy or whether you've caught a disease.

About Sex Definitions is a lengthy, but sometimes simplistic dictionary of sexual terms.

About Positions explains the pros and cons of the four basic positions: missionary, girl on top, side to side, and doggy-style.

About Contraception A brief, but clear guide to the different methods of contraception available.

About Aids/HIV contains clear, jargon-free information on how to safeguard against the HIV virus, as well as what it is and how it spreads.

About Anal Sex is a question-and-answer section, which provides sound advice in an open-minded and unpatronising manner, where even the most innocent questions are given a fully-detailed answer.

OTHER FEATURES

Sex Toys, Water Play, Masturbation, Sex Links, Homosexuality, Humor, Sex Pictures, The G-Spot, Fellatio, Cunnilingus and Condoms.

Comprehensive information about sex, presented in a frank and simple manner.

www.tantra.org and www.tantra.com

Church of Tantra and Tantra.com

overall rating:
★★★★
classification:
information
updated:
occasionally
navigation:
★★★★
content:
★★★★
readability:
★★★
orgasm rating:
not applicable
orgasm rating:
not applicable
speed:
★★★★
US

This is the website of the Church of Tantra, an ancient Indian philosophy which seeks to explore and develop sexuality as a spiritual force. Be warned: there are no quick-fix tips on how to attain the ultimate orgasm, but those seeking a deeper understanding of sexuality will find it a useful resource. Much of the information is presented in haiku-like poetry form, and though it may sound esoteric, once deciphered, it's down-to-earth advice. The site is sponsored by www.tantra.com, which takes a more westernised view of tantra as sexercise and applies the techniques and philosophies to modern sexual relationships. There are plenty of links between the two.

SPECIAL FEATURES

The Basis of Tantra is probably the most useful place to start for the novice devotee, explaining in simple terms the biological and philosophical basis of tantra.

OTHER FEATURES

An Overview of Tantra, Common Questions about Tantra Answered, Breath Control, Yoni Massage, and Lingam Massage.

An excellent introduction to the philosophy of tantra and tantric sex.

overall rating:
★★★★
classification:
service
updated:
frequently
navigation:
★★★
content:
★★★★★
readability:
★★★
orgasm rating:
not applicable
orgasm rating:
not applicable
speed:
★★★★
UK

http://www.informedconsent.co.uk

Informed Consent

Informed Consent is a free resource site for BDSM practitioners. It is dedicated to understanding and consensuality. It is a UK-orientated, non-commercial site. An immense amount of information is offered, and it is indispensable to newcomers on the UK BDSM scene. The presentation could be improved, and the main page is confusing in that it lists some links, but not all.

SPECIAL FEATURES

Informed Consent is an explanation of the world of erotic domination and submission. There is also important advice on safety limits and abuse.

Articles is a selection of contributors' articles explaining the intricacies of BDSM.

MasterSlave.org.uk is devoted to male-dominant/female-submissive relationships, and offers a range of resources.

OTHER FEATURES

UK Events, UK BDSM Directory, UK Events, World BDSM Links, Personals, discussion boards, chat, and news are also offered.

A crucial starting point for UK BDSM enthusiasts, especially newcomers. Impressive content, if hard to surf.

www.sexuality.org

Society for Human Sexuality

Part of the Sex Education Web Circle, the Society for Human Sexuality is a social and educational organisation, which aims to promote understanding and appreciation of sexual expression. The site is cosy in tone and educational in content, and appears to be aimed at a more emotionally mature market than those who simply want to get their rocks off. There is information to suit a wide range of sexual activities and tastes, but the bulk of the site is aimed at those who prefer simple vanilla sex, are aiming to improve it, and possibly want to experiment a bit more.

overall rating:
★★★★
classification:
specialist service
updated:
frequently
navigation:
★★★★★
content:
★★★★
readability:
★★★★
orgasm rating:
♀♀♀
orgasm rating:
♂♂♂
speed:
★★★★
US

SPECIAL FEATURES

Learning More is an information section covering everything from flirting to polyamory, as well as the archives of the 'Sexuality Advisor'.

Guides and Reviews contains reviews of sex education-related books and videos.

Sex Toys is a review section of sex aids, which reviews reputable brands, not only on the erotic pleasure they give, but on quality, tasteful packaging and respect for the customer as well.

A sensitive and informative site, for those who believe that sexuality and self-respect go hand in hand.

overall rating:
★★★
classification:
information
updated:
occasionally
navigation:
★★★
content:
★★★★
readability:
★★★★
orgasm rating:
♀♀♀♀
orgasm rating:
♂♂♂♂
speed:
★★★
US

http://www.proaxis.com/~solo

Solo

The Solo site approaches masturbation as a pleasurable and healthy pastime in its own right, rather than a poor relation to sex with someone else. The agenda of the site is three-fold: firstly, to dispel any guilt or misgivings you have regarding masturbation, then to get rid of some of the myths that surround the subject, and then finally to tell you how to do it better. The design of the site is uninspiring and scrappy-looking, though this is more than made up for by the quality of the content.

SPECIAL FEATURES

Why Masturbation is Good for You will give you all the excuses you ever needed to get started, explaining why it is good for your health and how it can improve your sex life.

Here's How I Do It is a considerable archive of Tips and Techniques, sent in by readers. The content is largely unedited, which makes it seem slightly amateurish, but also allows the unbiased experiences of real people to shine through.

Showing Off is another archive compiled of personal (and supposedly true) erotic masturbation stories sent in by readers, as well as a video exchange and contacts list.

A useful archive if you want to know more about the ins and outs of masturbation.

Section 02

for starters

All good things lead from here. So do a lot of bad things, but hopefully with the tips given, these shouldn't be too hard to avoid.

Usually, the easiest way to search for what you want is to use a search engine, such as Lycos or Altavista. These allow you put in key words and then produce a list of sites in which the words are found. This system works a lot better if you are trying to buy a stuffed aardvark then if you are trying to find a sex site. Paysites put a lot of effort into luring you in, and are often stuffed full of sex related keywords and special pages designed to be found by search engines. Try feeding in 'sex, naked, girls' as keywords and see what happens! Conversely, smaller, interesting sites will often not be listed at all.

A far better way is to choose a site that specialises in sex site listings. There are plenty of these, and although they tend to include banners advertising paysites, most are staunch supporters of free net sex. For those who simply want a plentiful supply of dirty pictures with no hassle, this is the best route to take. Our favourites: www.drbizzaro.com and www.persiankitty.com, are reviewed along with some more specialist choices.

Once you have found a few good sites life becomes easier. Most sites include links to related sites, which in turn contain further links, so you can quickly build a list of favourites.

overall rating:
★★★★★
classification:
links site
updated:
daily
navigation:
★★★★★
content:
★★★★
readability:
★★★
orgasm rating:
♀
orgasm rating:
♂♂♂♂
speed:
★★★★
US

http://www.persiankitty.com

Persian Kitty

A big, well-presented, user-friendly links site. Persian Kitty is perhaps the best known jumping-off point for porn surfers, listing hundreds of sites which in turn give access to innumerable pictures, stories, chatrooms, and so forth. The emphasis is on free sites, although many of these are introductions to paysites. Navigating around the site is easy, and slowed only by its sheer volume. Getting to what you really want to see is often rather less easy, although it is all there. The style of the site is friendly, open and welcoming to both sexes and all sexualities, although it is mainly aimed at straight, heterosexual men.

SPECIAL FEATURES

Free Sites Listings This is the heart of Persian Kitty, an extensive list of free sex sites, supplying links to as much straightforward porn as any visitor could possibly want, from Aaron's All Star Hooters to Zara Zakova's Russian Teens. It is not overwhelmed by banners, but it may take a little patience to make it work for you. Sites are listed by title, along with the number of pictures they contain and whether thumbnail images are supplied.

Categorised Sites Listings Sites not listed in the main area are categorised here and less frequently updated. As well as paysites, these include picture sites for fetishists and gay men, sites for stories, toys and clothing, chat, advice, web cams, and more; really anything whatever related to sex. A useful feature is that current prices are listed for all paysites.

PK's Thumbnail Gallery Post provides direct links to thumbnailed galleries for those impatient to get to the pictures. Again, the content is largely softcore/hardcore. New sites are added every few days, and listed in order of appearance.

PK's Exclusive Free Pics A detail, but a nice one, with one exceptional picture and one naughty panoramic background for your wallpaper each day.

PK's Voice Chat is a new feature, enabling visitors to chat by voice, for free.

OTHER FEATURES

Persian Kitty also offers visitors the chance to submit or update links, download banners, and comment on the site.

A well-presented, comprehensive starting point. Perfect for the porn-surfer-in-the-street.

overall rating:
★★★★★
classification:
commercial resource
updated:
daily
navigation:
★★★★
content:
★★★★★
readability:
★★★★★
orgasm rating:
♀♀♀♀
orgasm rating:
♂♂♂♂♂
speed:
★★★★★
US

http://www.pictureview.com

Pictureview

A simple, straightforward resource site and much the best way to view what's on the newsgroups. For $8 per month you can view daily updated thumbnail galleries from an enormous range of newsgroups (not just sex-related ones). Signing ontonewsgroups may theoretically give unlimited free access to sexy pictures on every topic imaginable, but the reality is somewhat different. Firstly, newsgroups carry an enormous amount of spam, which makes accessing them tedious at the best of times. Postings of pictures also frequently come in sections and may carry viruses, making it slow and dangerous to get what you want. Pictureview overcomes these problems, and probably saves more money than it costs just in terms of time. The sheer volume of newsgroups can make navigation tricky, but we had fun with it anyway. Non-members can access galleries but not full-sized pictures. The very lack of discrimination makes the site worthwhile for everyone, so long as you like dirty pictures. This is why we have given the sight a high orgasm rating despite it being primarily a jumpsite.

Warning: Pictureview does its best not to include illegal and copyrighted images, yet the input is direct from newsgroups, and detailed censorship is impossible. You may not like what you see.

SPECIAL FEATURES

Newsgroup Listings This is the principal function of Pictureview, listing several hundred newsgroups by URL. Each lists the number of pictures available and the number added during the day. There may be a handful, there may be thousands. Clicking on the newsgroup title will take you to one or more thumbnail galleries and in turn to the pictures themselves. The variety is extraordinary, although we found that the actual content didn't always match the title. Just a few of the newgroups included are:

alt.binaries.erotica.pornstar
alt.binaries.erotica.voyeurism.hiddencamera
alt.binaries.pictures.erotica.bikerchicks
alt.binaries.pictures.erotica.gaymen
alt.binaries.pictures.erotica.fetish.female.socks
alt.binaries.pictures.erotica.chastity-belt
alt.binaries.pictures.erotica.male.bodybuilder
alt.binaries.pictures.erotica.transexual.action
alt.sex.fetish.tickling

and many, many more. Within all of these we found the good, the bad and the ugly, but be assured, you get what you click on!

OTHER FEATURES

Pictureview also offers a free demo and a guide to the site. Warnings and mission statements are included, along with links to Net Nanny and Cyber Patrol.

The best way to surf the newsgroups. Excellent value for once!

overall rating:
★★★★
classification:
links site
updated:
frequently
navigation:
★★★★★
content:
★★★★
readability:
★★★★★
orgasm rating:
♀♀♀
orgasm rating:
♂♂♂
speed:
★★★★
US

http://www.fetishbank.net

Bank of Fetish Resources

The Bank of Fetish Resources is a free, extensively categorised jumpstation for fetishists of every possible type. The only categories excluded are the blatantly illegal, while an attempt is made to be truly comprehensive. Visitors are even invited to suggest new categories. The style is detached, even clinical. Sites are divided into three main areas: softcore, hardcore, and extreme, along with warnings for the unwary. The presentation is simple, clear, and easy to use, with a minimum of commercial banners. Within each category, sites are further subdivided, covering sites with pictures and those dedicated to stories, chat, links, and contacts, as well as related sites. Once inside, it is sometimes hard to sort free sites from commercial ones, and the listings, while good, are by no means comprehensive.

SPECIAL FEATURES

The Fetish Bank front page invites entry to two main areas: Enter Bank and Enter TGP (Thumbnail Gallery Post). These give access to the site listings and listings of free galleries respectively. The format within each area is the same.

Softcore features ordinary porn and lighter fetishes. These are precisely divided, with even the most straightforward smut being divided according to hair colour and race. Most categories are commonplace, for instance celebrities, porn stars, exhibitionism, and large and small breasts. Others are more specialist, such as wet sex, wrestling, uniforms and hairy girls. A few are highly specialised such as valkyries, pie-fighting, and balloons, and no we don't mean large breasts, we mean balloons!

Hardcore Basically defined as contact sex, hardcore categories include plain old fucking and sucking, along with anal sex and what are so sweetly described as facials. Harder fetishes are also covered. Bondage, spanking, and mild erotic tortures are included, along with clothing fetishes, transvestism, and sex toy play.

Extreme features those categories that break society's strongest sexual taboos, dealing with subjects such as bestiality, bodily functions, and medical fetishism. This is beyond what many would consider acceptable, and caution is advised.

Daily Updates is a choice of direct links to pictures, updated daily and drawn from a selection of categories. A useful area for quick access to high-quality pictures.

OTHER FEATURES

A few recommendations are made, care advised, and limited shopping opportunities offered.

An indispensable site for those with broadly fetishistic tastes, good for the curious, but less so for single-fetish fanatics.

overall rating:
★★★★
classification:
links site
updated:
frequently
navigation:
★★★
content:
★★★★
readability:
★★★
orgasm rating:
♀♀♀
orgasm rating:
♂♂♂♂
speed:
★★★★
US

http://drbizzaro.com/main.html

DrBizzarro.com

Dr Bizzaro's is an exceptional free listings site and more besides. Links are divided into 16 categories, and lead to picture listings or thumbnail galleries, as well as movies and stories. These cover a broad range of subjects, including listings for the more common specialist tastes, such as women in panties. Gay listings are included, but as a minority feature. Many other features are included, while the site is constantly policed by the Doctor to remove dead or altered links. The presentation is detailed but cluttered simply because there is so much content. Updates are frequent, and those categories to which new links have been added are marked. The site is reasonably fast and contains no more banners than might be expected. It is important to note the correct spelling, DrBizzaro.com, as this site is sufficiently popular to have spawned imitators, many of them commercial. The Doctor's style is friendly and less laddish than many similar sites, although those who try to abuse the system are given grief in turn.

SPECIAL FEATURES

Shopping Sex toys can be ordered online from an impressively large range, from anal beads to vibrating nipples clamps, and they are all neatly categorised for ease of purchase. Videos are also available, although the range is less extensive.

Amateur Galleries These have been a long running feature of the site, presenting pictures sent in by users, which are generally of themselves. They are divided into two groups; one for women alone and couples, and one for men alone and gay men. Inevitably, the content is varied in quality, but such galleries do provide an intimacy lacking in commercial photographs and video captures.

Hardcore Hospital An internal paysite featuring a large collection of selected pictures, movies, stories, and chatrooms. This is extensive and well constructed, but very much for the true sex-surf addict.

Blacklist A frequently updated list of sites which have abused the doctor's hospitality, mainly by resetting gallery links to large commercial banner farms. Sites that have failed to pay for the inclusion of their advertising banners are also included.

OTHER FEATURES

Archives boasts extensive archives, providing links to many thousands of pictures, while Traffic Referrals lists other similar sites that the Doctor considers worthwhile, along with a table of referral popularity. Guest Book may be signed by visitors, and provides the Doctor with comments on his site.

One of the top sex links sites, with easy access to all the smut you could ever want.

overall rating:
★★★★
classification:
webring
updated:
frequently
navigation:
★★★★
content:
★★★★
readability:
★★★
orgasm rating:
♀♀♀♀
orgasm rating:
♂♂♂
speed:
★★★★
US

http://www.webring.org/cgi-bin/webring?ring=eroticartring;list

Erotic Art Webring

The Erotic Art Webring is a free listing that presents over 140 erotic art sites. It is a useful resource for anybody interested in the subject, and includes sites almost regardless of content, from the very softest to extremely strong. Gentle pastel and charcoal nudes that could be shown to Great Aunt Hilda are followed by extreme BDSM and sex with aliens. Unfortunately, there is no editing for quality, which means that while most art featured is of a good standard and some very fine indeed, some is truly abysmal. The site descriptions are written by the individual hosts, making it hard to pick the good from the bad and sometimes to read at all. Many sites offer artwork for sale or on commission. Other list sites are also included.

SPECIAL FEATURES

Over 140 are listed, split into eight pages. Some examples are considered separately, while others include:

Alphafox Illustration Erotic furry art by Matt Willard, featuring anthropomorphic foxes, both male and female.

Art Concepts Soft semi-nudes in chalk pastels.

Dushi's BDSM Art A well-presented site featuring the work of BDSM artists which, aside from a small preview area, is accessible to contributors only.

Erotic Art Top 100 Websites is a listing site for mainly commercial porn-art collections.

Female Domination and Face Sitting Drawings Fantasy is exactly what it says, showing full, luscious women sitting on men's faces. Quite small, good cartoon-style art.

Pin-up Girls is a site featuring over 600 pin-up girl images.

RaineyzArt features customised erotic pottery.

Shystar's Sketchbook of Original Homo and Hetero Art Largely homoerotic artwork.

Kafenwar's Lush Ladies is the work of an artist specialising in voluptuous women.

World Art Erotica Human sexuality displayed in both art and literature. A members' site, but with a free preview section.

OTHER FEATURES

A word search facility is offered, as well as the chance to join the ring or go to the main Webring homepage.

A great starting point when searching for erotic art.

overall rating:
★★★★
classification:
service
updated:
frequently
navigation:
★★★★★
content:
★★★★
readability:
★★★★
orgasm rating:
♀♀♀
orgasm rating:
♂♂♂
speed:
★★★★
US

http://www.janesguide.com

Jane's Net Sex Guide

Jane's Guide is a US site specialising in reviews of sex-related websites. They cover the whole range of sex-related topics, from straightforward picture galleries to tantric sex advice. The emphasis is on US sites, but the Guide has worldwide coverage and regional guides for relevant topics. The site is fast and easy to use, detailed in some areas, and rather spartan in others.

SPECIAL FEATURES

Jane's Guide is broken down into nine sections:

Primarily Photos features reviews of sites that focus on picture galleries. It is broken down into 19 sub-categories according to the types of photo. We looked at Big, Beautiful Women (women who self-identify as big. In practice, most are average). Thirty-eight reviews were listed, which should keep anyone happy.

Fetish and BDSM covers all types of sites focusing on this area. We had a look at the spanking category and found only 10 reviews, with many of the most popular sites not covered.

Online Video includes reviews of individual women's webcams, live cams, and live streaming.

Services reviews sites for personals, phonesex, postcards, and link sites; a rather diffuse category.

The Written Word is a section for magazines, erotica, advice, and anything else presented as text.

Resources covers resource sites for the full width of sexual matters including BDSM, gay male, bisexual, lesbian, transgender, sex work, safety, and family-planning issues.

Products to Purchase features reviews of online shops for any sex-related products. There is a strong US bias here, although some UK stores are covered.

Miscellany covers anything else, from sex-positive goddesses to Jane's bookmarks and more.

Regional Guide features reviews of those sites where region matters: escort services, massage, swinging, BDSM groups, strip clubs, professional domination, and so on. We found the UK section worthwhile if far from comprehensive.

Articles provides information to surfers; for instance, a well-written and useful article discussing and comparing adult verification services.

OTHER FEATURES

Jane's Guide also provides chat, a daily journal, discussion boards, and Jane's webcam.

A starting point that will take you just about anywhere, but maybe not directly.

overall rating:
★★★★
classification:
specialist service
updated:
frequently
navigation:
★★★★★
content:
★★★★
readability:
★★★★
orgasm rating:
not applicable
orgasm rating:
not applicable
speed:
★★★★
US

http://www.top100-uk-swingers.com

Top 100 UK Swingers

Top 100 UK Swingers is a listing dedicated to the UK swingers' scene. Despite the title, we found only 28 sites listed, with a total of 49 in their searchable database. Doubtless they will get to the one hundred mark in due time. The site is completely matter-of-fact, listing all sites relevant to the UK swingers' scene in order of the number of hits that have come in from them. The layout and navigation are absolutely straightforward and the speed good. There were only two advertising banners.

SPECIAL FEATURES

Toplist is the central feature of the site, presenting banner links for the top ten sites and simpler links for the remainder. Emma and Carl's UK-Swapscene topped the list and is reviewed separately. The other sites include specialist swinging sites and more general contact sites. We had a look at ABC Dating and Personals, which ranked second, finding a straightforward contact site affiliated to the one-and-only.com system, which is a vast database with a rather simple search system. ABC also offer a fantasy match facility for fetishists and various services and products. Among other sites some were free, while others charged a membership fee. Several offered facilities to fetishists and BDSMers as well as swingers. None was specifically gay. One escort service was listed, which we didn't really feel belonged here.

OTHER FEATURES

Links are also offered to swinging sites and listings outside the UK. There is a database search facility, a webmaster's lounge, and a list of those sites they include but who refuse to display their banner.

An ideal starting point for all UK-based swingers.

overall rating:
★★★
classification:
links
updated:
occasionally
navigation:
★★★
content:
★★★
readability:
★★
orgasm rating:
not applicable
orgasm rating:
not applicable
speed:
★★★★
US

http://nav.webring.org

WebRing

WebRing is the umbrella site for individual webrings, each dedicated to a particular subject. This is the largest of several similar sites, and covers not just erotica, but the full spectrum of topics available on the net. To reach the erotic listings, find Society and Culture near the bottom of the main page, then click on Sexuality. This will take you to the main erotic sites listing. The service is completely free and certainly extensive. When we visited, over 400 individual webrings were listed, with an average of perhaps 30 sites each. Unfortunately, this does not mean easy access to 12,000 worthwhile sites; many are duplicated, while many of what appear to be good sites will prove to be entrances to paysites or banner-farms, and others will be dead links. It is, nonetheless, the sheer volume of the links that makes it a worthwhile starting point. Proceed with caution and patience.

SPECIAL FEATURES

With no editing or rationalisation, and sites listed according to whatever their owners want to say, webrings possess all the anarchy that is both the curse and the blessing of the internet. We looked at the listings with a mixture of delight and exasperation, finding, among others:

$ Totally Free Adult Sites $ Great, you might think, but not when it lists only five members and is one of well over a dozen similar webrings. We tried a few, and while some work, more directed us to dubious money-making schemes: huge banner farms of 'free' sites demanding credit card details for entry.

Spanking Internet's Webring listed 96 separate sites when we visited. Unfortunately, it is only one of at least seven spanking webrings, with no real differentiation between them. Meanwhile the Giant Spanking Webring lists only 19 sites.

GayChange Webring is a Christian webring devoted to changing unwanted same-sex attraction and acknowledging the transforming power of Jesus Christ as Lord and God of all creation, and also of our sexuality. Well fair enough, if that's what you want, but it's hardly erotica.

OTHER FEATURES

WebRing provides word search facilities, support, and information, which are all accessible from the main page.

Effectively a gigantic but indiscriminate listing of websites, erotic included.

Section 03

erotica

The internet is an excellent forum for erotic artists. As the subject tends to be shunned by the art establishment, the net is ideal for those who want to promote their work without censorship or interference. Unfortunately, this freedom means that much of what is available on the net is of abysmal quality. The net is also the natural forum for computer-enhanced art.

What makes good erotic art is a highly subjective question. In general, we have aimed for the stimulating and avoided the pretentious. In the art world, cartoon art and fantasy art are seen as inferior to fine art. For erotic art the opposite is generally the case, and while we have gone for technically skilled artists we have not avoided any particular style. What we have avoided are images depicting acts of extreme violence and sadism, which are regrettably common on the net. We have allowed some images that would not be acceptable as photographs. A picture of a girl having sex with an anthropomorphic cartoon walrus is so inherently ludicrous that it hardly counts as bestiality.

A major section of erotic art on the net comes from Japanese cartoons. The content of these varies from soft to unacceptably extreme. A few terms are worth knowing; in practice, these are often used incorrectly.

Anime: Animation with a distinctive Japanese drawing style.

Manga: Comic books in the same style.

Ecchi: Anime or Manga with adult content. Literally 'indecent'.
Hentai: Anime or Manga with adult content. Literally 'transformation' or 'perversion'.

These terms are often used interchangeably to describe art in the Anime style, with body contours both simplified and exaggerated, brilliant but unlikely hair colours, and a broadly science-fantasy feel. Japanese censorship laws mean that the genitals are often obscured or missing entirely, leading to some very peculiar effects. These styles are now spreading, and US and UK versions are increasingly common.

BDSM pictures are also common on the net and again often exceed the bounds of acceptability. The style tends to be related to the country of origin, with bondage and watersports from Japan, spanking and female domination from the UK, and All American imagery from the US.

Many of the pictures available on the net are scanned from hardcopy publications and presented without copyright permission, which is a widespread problem on the net. How much this promotes the artists and how much it prevents them from making a living is debatable, but for this reason many of the best artists' sites present their pictures only in small format to prevent them being stolen. Free sites are relatively common with artwork and scams are relatively rare.

overall rating:
★★★★★
classification:
ezine
updated:
monthly
navigation:
★★★★★
content:
★★★★★
readability:
★★★★
orgasm rating:
♀♀♀♀♀
orgasm rating:
♂♂♂
speed:
★★★★
US

www.erotica-readers.com

Erotic Readers Association

Sites like the Erotic Readers Association are a welcome oasis in the sea of smut which exists in cyberspace. Where other sites promise a kinder, gentler style of erotica, then fail to deliver, the Erotic Readers Association succeeds, with a sizeable selection of erotic fiction, poetry, and features on offer. The contributors to the site have very different styles, but all have a sharp wit, with the ability to bring out the humour of sex without detracting from the erotic style. The site is primarily aimed at women, but not exclusively so, and has several male contributors to the messageboards and archives.

Pre-Raphaelite illustrations decorate the site throughout and impart a romantic character to the site, and a picture of Eve, tempts you into the main sections.

SPECIAL FEATURES

Galleries There are five galleries of erotic fiction which range from Flashers of 100 words, to full-length stories. The Feature Gallery has a special theme which changes every two months. The feature for the summer was Sex Toys and included an adult version of Toy Story, with the Buzz and Woody characters re-invented as vibrators vying for their mistress' attention. Once the theme changes the stories are archived in the Treasure Chest section, which is further sub-divided into Hetero-erotica, Quickies, The Softer Side, BDSM, Lesbian, and Bisexual.

Book Reviews and Recommendations includes a useful guide to erotica, which briefly explains the history and genres of the subject.

Author's Library contains everything the budding erotic writer needs to know to write, sell, and publish erotic works, with articles on writing techniques which ponder such questions as 'Come and Cum: which is the correct spelling?'

Inside the Erotic Mind is a series of messageboards, featuring discussions on all aspects of sexuality and sexual politics, including such debates as: 'Is Cybersex Adultery?', 'BDSM: Pleasurable Pain?' and 'Erotica vs.Porn'. The contributions are are thoughtful, articulate, and open-minded. You can contribute to any discussion by clicking on Participate at the bottom of the page. If you want to remain anonymous, you can simply omit your name and email address.

OTHER FEATURES

Cinema Wing, Smutter's Lounge, and Musical Masterpieces.

Lots of high-quality erotica for erotic readers and writers.

overall rating:
★★★★★
classification:
homepage
updated:
frequently
navigation:
★★★
content:
★★★★★
readability:
★★★★★
orgasm rating:
♀♀
orgasm rating:
♂♂♂
speed:
★★★
US

http://www.geocities.com/FashionAvenue/Salon/4039

Pin-up Girls – The Pin-up Art Archive

An archive of US pin-up art hosted by Kabarl. This, he says, is a labour of love, and it is a pretty impressive one. The content is exclusively classic US pin-up art, the soft erotic imagery, clothed or semi-nude, on which so many people grew up from the thirties well into the sixties. Kabarl intends this as a complete resource for pin-up art fans, and it is certainly more than a simply gallery site. The design is good, but the navigation imperfect, with inconsistent internal links. The sheer size of the site makes it slow, but it is banner-free and very readable. By modern standards the art is sexist to say the least, but we liked it anyway.

SPECIAL FEATURES

Artists is the heart of the site, listing 17 artists and over 600 pictures when we visited. Each artist is given a brief biography followed by a thumbnail gallery of their work. The most famous of these is undoubtedly Alberto Vargas, the Esquire and Playboy artist whose wholesome, smiling girls define what the majority of people think of as pin-up art. His girls come in a wide variety of poses, nude, semi-nude or clothed, but always with the passive, winsome eroticism that characterises his work. Art Frahm created little scenarios rather than simple poses, his great speciality being 'damsels in distress': girls who had lost their knickers in some awkward and embarrassing situation. Pearl Frush was one of the handful of female pin-up artists. Her subjects are similar to those of Vargas, this being the style in demand at the time, but her work is firmer, more detailed, certainly as skilled, and perhaps more evocative. We liked the picture of the girl happily sweeping up in just her pinny. Blatant sexism? Submissive female imagery? Maybe both, but it must be remembered that Frush, like all these artists, was a child of her time.

Bookstore provides links to Amazon and Amazon UK, and recommends a selection of pin-up art books, each with a text link to the relevant page on Amazon.

OTHER FEATURES

A message board, a word search facility, a guestbook, links, and a chatroom are also provided.

A great resource for all fans of US pin-up art.

overall rating:
★★★★★
classification:
artist's homepage
updated:
monthly
navigation:
★★★★★
content:
★★★★★
readability:
★★★★★
orgasm rating:
♀♀♀♀
orgasm rating:
♂♂♂♂
speed:
★★★
UK

http://easyweb.easynet.co.uk/~sartopia

Sartopia

The homepage of the artist known as Sardax, often considered the UK's top female domination artist. His work is skilled and detailed, sometimes extraordinarily so. Women are magnificent Amazons, while men skinny, inadequate creatures usually grovelling on the ground. The site is a showcase for this work, a broad range of which is presented in thumbnailed galleries. It is free, well designed, and easy to navigate and read, if not particularly fast. A must for those who enjoy the imagery of female domination, and worth looking at even if you like the opposite.

SPECIAL FEATURES

Sartopia lists eight areas accessible from text links on the mainpage:

Fantasies is a gallery of 12 thumbnailed Sardax pictures. Each is a different female domination fantasy. Many have an oriental feel, but he covers just about every dominant female image that has ever been thought up, and takes a dominant slant on many that would normally be considered submissive.

Leg Show features his work for a US magazine devoted to foot and leg fetishism, but with an element of female domination. These pictures come from US sexual imagery (the trailer park slut, the cheerleader, the professional dominatrix), and concentrate on legs, feet and the male perspective of a woman as viewed from ground level.

Alice Kerr Sutherland Society features Sardax's work for this UK female domination society, which claims to be the most elegant and refined journal of disciplinary literature in the world. These are technically soft, but powerfully erotic within their context.

Other Works is an annotated selection of other works, including personal commissions.

Sketches contains examples of less polished work on the same themes.

Shanghai Bizarre features illustrations from a forthcoming book based on his world of complex and bizarre female domination scenarios and inspired by the work of Nimrod, another aficionado of female domination. The telephone exchange with men enclosed in the seats so that the female operator spends the day sitting on their faces is a classic example of the artist's imagination.

Words The artist's background and philosophy of life.

OTHER FEATURES

Links are provided to other female domination-related websites. Artwork may be commissioned, and Sardax emailed directly.

The homepage of the UK's best known female domination artist.

overall rating:
★★★★★
classification:
homepage/membership
updated:
frequently
navigation:
★★★★
content:
★★★★★
readability:
★★★★
orgasm rating:
♀♀♀
orgasm rating:
♂♂♂♂♂
speed:
★★★
US £

http://spiritworks-art.com

The Spirit's Visual Arts Studio

This is the gallery site of 'The Spirit', an artist who really understands the nuances of erotic display, especially when it involves his favourite subject, spanking pretty girls. His beautifully rendered cartoons capture the emotion of the subjects as few other artists can. We have two regrets: first that, being American, more British themes aren't covered; and second, that there isn't more, and more and more... Despite this, we both adored the site, and if you enjoy the thoroughly Old English pleasure of spanking a bare bottom, we're sure you will too, girl or boy. The site is beautifully designed, well presented, and easy to browse. Free galleries are provided as well as the members' area. The site costs $14.95 for a month or $39.95 for three months.

SPECIAL FEATURES

Free Galleries is a thumbnail presentation of The Spirit's art, each thumbnail leading to a full-sized picture. These are samples from some of his best work, and they offer more than just a taster, with the emphasis placed firmly on erotic spanking. There is also a small preview section for the members' area.

Once Upon a Spanking features several thumbnailed galleries of The Spirit's best spanking art. We loved the way each picture conveys the emotion and erotic tension of the moment.

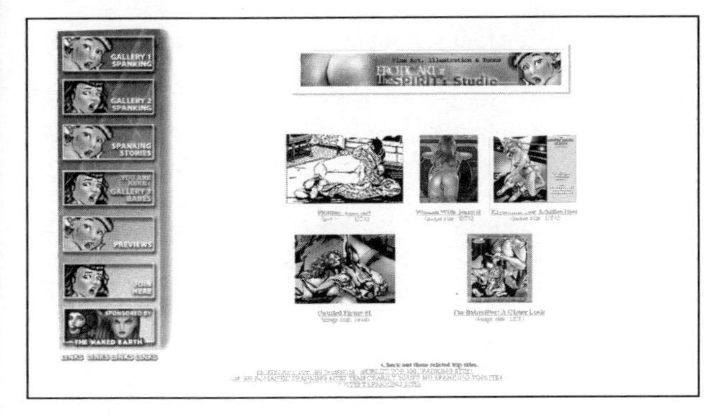

Babes in Dreamland The Spirit's more general art, including erotic display and the rarer fantasies of wrestling between girls and tickling. Again, he captures the moment to perfection.

Shopping provides a chance to buy The Spirit's erotic art or commission more.

OTHER FEATURES

Links to related sites, a biography of the artist, and a what's new section are also provided.

A showcase for a top erotic artist specialising in emotionally powerful images of female submission.

overall rating:
★★★★
classification:
portal
updated:
frequently
navigation:
★★★
content:
★★★★★
readability:
★★★
orgasm rating:
♀♀♀♀
orgasm rating:
♂♂♂♂
speed:
★★★
US

www.asstr.org

alt.sex.stories

This site receives a four-star rating for sheer volume. It is host to over 200 sites for authors of erotica, plus the alt.sex.stories. moderated newsgroup. As with any site with so many contributors, the quality is variable: ranging from amateurish recollections to eloquent literature. Unfortunately, there is no sample text to give you an indication of this, and finding the best stories appears to be a process of trial and error. However, many of the authors have a decent-sized archive, so once you've found an author that you like you can always go back for more.

The homepage is plain and text-heavy with minimal graphics, and it can be cumbersome to find your way around, though it's simple enough to search for stories. To search, choose from the selection of new stories on the right-hand side of the homepage, or search by author or keyword. Clicking on the author's heading on the left-hand side of the homepage takes you through to a table of authors. From here you can click straight through to their website, or have a look at their profile to get an idea of their writing style. Once you've read a story, you'll have to use the browser's back button to get back to the asstr homepage.

SPECIAL FEATURES

There is a huge number of erotic writers, but not so many good ones. Here's a small selection to get you started:

Adhara is an astrophysics student, and science makes its way into several of her erotic stories. Don't let that put you off though; it's surprising how sexy flying electrons can be in the heat of the moment. Her name features on several other US-based erotica sites, including Clean Sheets (see p55.), but a small collection of her earlier work can be found here. The stories are short and beautifully written, and though the site hasn't been updated since 1999, the quality of what is there makes it worth a visit.

Sarah H. specialises in mind-control erotica, and many stories explore the dark side of the emotions, with participants struggling against unseen forces, then succumbing and losing control. The stories can be harsh and sometimes cruel, but successfully convey the power of sex as a weapon. Even the author admits that some of the scenarios she portrays would be considered highly unethical in real life, but reading about such raw emotions can still be erotic and strangely cathartic.

Ann Douglas has produced a substantial collection of stories dating from 1993, on a number of themes, including historical, sci-fi as well as contemporary heterosexual and girl to girl.

Don't be put off by the lack of visual creativity at this site; if you're prepared to rummage around, there are *some gems to be had.*

overall rating:
★★★★
classification:
homepage
updated:
occasionally
navigation:
★★★★
content:
★★★★
readability:
★★★★★
orgasm rating:
♀♀♀
orgasm rating:
♂♂♂
speed:
★★★★
US

http://dsoft.minx.nu/main.html

Dsoft erotic toons

Jessica Rabbit nude? Alice in a threesome with Tweedledee and Tweedledum? Then this is the site for you. It's strange, there's no denying it, but if eroticised cartoons are your thing, then this is an excellent site. It's free, reasonably fast with few banners, and well presented, with around 1,000 pictures. These are thumbnailed and vary in quality. Most are drawn from widely recognised cartoons owned by Disney and Warner Brothers, while others are from purely US cartoons, which may dull the impact and humour for British surfers. These vary from clearly erotic images such as Jessica Rabbit, to the frankly surreal, such as eroticised geese. The bulk of the content is soft, but can be very strong, yet we felt that the inevitable flavour of the absurd saved these from being unacceptable.

SPECIAL FEATURES

Seventeen galleries are currently on display, which include:

Esmerelda the gipsy girl from Quasimodo, displayed in a wide variety of rude poses, mostly alone, and surprisingly few with her grotesque co-star.

Daphne the cheerleader type from Scooby Doo, again mainly naked or half dressed and in poses typical of the cartoon.

Jessica Rabbit the vamp from Who Framed Roger Rabbit? in all her naked glory, impossibly bouyant bust and all.

Gosalyn the sexy duck? Surely too strange to appeal to all but the most unworldly of fetishists.

OTHER FEATURES

In addition to the pictures, there are links to similar sites, news, and a chance to email or make donations. The site is a member of both the Erotic Art Webring and the Cartoon Webring, which are linked.

Popular cartoon characters in erotic form, weird but wonderful.

overall rating:
★★★★
classification:
artist's homepage
updated:
occasionally
navigation:
★★★★★
content:
★★★★
readability:
★★★★★
orgasm rating:
♀♀♀
orgasm rating:
♂♂♂
speed:
★★★
US

http://www.sfo.com/~mack/eros

Erotic Art by Ryan Mack

This is the homepage of Ryan Mack, a California-based artist. Mack provides a good example of an artist producing computer-derived works, in this case with adobe imaging software. The site is well designed, opening with a jumpstation designed around one of the artist's pictures. It was somewhat slow, but with a frank, open style, and was free of advertising banners and other annoyances. There could have been more artwork, but doubtless that will come in time.

SPECIAL FEATURES

Galleries Two galleries are presented: Alone, covering single female nudes, and Together, covering couples, mainly women with women. The pictures are presented as thumbnails, with each one leading to a larger picture. Most of these appear to derive from pictures that are available on the net, but have been adapted to create a style that is at once sensual and provocative. Each picture is named. We looked at Time for Bondage, a bound and gagged female figure in erotic clothing set against a distorted checkerboard and rendered entirely in black and white.

About the Artist features a brief biography of the artist. We felt that there could have been more.

Shows In the past Ryan Mack has held public exhibitions of his work, but none was scheduled when we visited.

OTHER FEATURES

Prints may be purchased direct from the artist. Ordering details are provided, and it is possible to join the mailing list. There is a guestbook, and a limited selection of links are provided, though not necessarily to erotic art-related sites.

A site displaying good examples of computer-generated erotic art.

overall rating:
★★★★
classification:
free gallery
updated:
monthly
navigation:
★★★★
content:
★★★★★
readability:
★★★★
orgasm rating:
♀♀♀♀
orgasm rating:
♂♂♂♂
speed:
★★★
CANADA

http://freecartoonsex.com

Freecartoonsex.com

A big, free site for lovers of weird and wonderful cartoons. Freecartoonsex has a fairly international feel, with US, Japanese, and English cartoons, among others. The content varies from soft to very hard, but we felt the cartoon format saved it from the edge, along with the playful, tongue-in-cheek feel to the site. There are rather a lot of banners, which made navigation and readability tricky, especially as the important links tend to appear at the bottom of the page. The content is great though, just so long as you are into cartoon characters indulging in often improbable sex acts. Over 1,000 are included, all thumbnailed. A little slow.

SPECIAL FEATURES

The site has six main gallery areas: Anime Series, Hentai Series, Famous Toons, English Mangas, Japanese Mangas, and Artists. Famous Toons, which splits into fifteen sub-categories, was the one that we tried. Some, like Lara Croft, are clearly sexual, while others are less so, like the Simpsons or the Flintstones. We could just about handle the Teenage Mutant Ninja Turtles having group sex with April, but found the Warner Brothers characters a bit too much, though they were quite funny. Trying English Mangas, we found 19 galleries, mainly Fairie Fetish and Hot Tails. These are cartoon strips, and nothing if not imaginative. Fairie Fetish involves tiny (but mature) winged fairies, mainly girls, indulging themselves in their miniature world, with each

other, with caterpillars, and with a praying mantis. It's strange, but we must confess that we loved it.

OTHER FEATURES

Movies, support and links are also offered.

A great free site for sexy cartoons. A hit if it's your thing.

overall rating:
★★★★
classification:
artist's homepage
updated:
occasionally
navigation:
★★★★
content:
★★★
readability:
★★★
orgasm rating:
♀♀
orgasm rating:
♂♂♂
speed:
★★★★
SWEDEN

http://www.gutart.rit.se

GutArt Gallery

This is the homepage of the distinctive and original artist Heinz Guth. Guth specialises in erotic studies of large women (referred to throughout the site as BBWs – big, beautiful women) which he calls GutArt. The style is exotic and colourful, and we felt the site warranted inclusion not just for the quality of his painting, but for individuality and for daring to present such an unfashionable subject. The style is personal and open, and the presentation is good if perhaps a little fussy for easy navigation, with information in frames that are sometimes cramped. It is as readable as can be expected from a Swedish artist writing in English. This is a specialist site, but we thoroughly enjoyed our visit. The site is entirely free and has no paysite banners.

SPECIAL FEATURES

Galleries Forty-three galleries were listed when we visited, and more are added all the time. The majority are soft erotic, centred on women but including men. Information is included with all of them. The compositions are complex and imaginative, with imagery drawn from various sources, including Christian and Scandinavian mythology. Many galleries consist of one painting, with the finished product shown alongside preliminary sketches, the work at various stages, features and enlarged details. We looked at Angel – Heaven and Hell, a composition centred on a naked, voluptuous female angel along with various lesser figures, including the artist as one of the devils peering from behind the angel's wing. Whether this picture is erotic, disturbing or incomprehensible will be a matter of taste. The drawings galleries show a simpler, looser style, with big, beautiful women depicted naked or lightly clothed. Many of these had a light, summery feel, although some could only be considered erotic in an abstract sense. Other galleries include cartoons and illustrations for stories.

About Gut Art features information about the artist, his background, awards, and exhibitions

OTHER FEATURES

The artist's work is offered, both in original form and on CD, and exhibitions are advertised. A few links are provided, mainly to other sites with an interest in big women. Comments are welcomed.

An original homepage from an artist specialising in big, beautiful women.

overall rating:
★★★★
classification:
artist's homepage
updated:
occasionally
navigation:
★★★★
content:
★★★★
readability:
★★★★
orgasm rating:
♀♀♀
orgasm rating:
♂♂♂♂
speed:
★★★★★
ITALY

http://www.milomanara.com

The Official Milo Manara Website

Milo Manara is without doubt one of the world's leading erotic artists, blending artistic skill with sensuous, often quirky imagery. There is plenty of his work on the net, mainly without thought for copyright, but this is his official site. This is entirely free, well designed, in frames, very fast, and illustrated with examples of his work. English and Italian language choices are given. The samples are presented one by one, rather than in galleries, and they are not particularly large, but for anyone who enjoys erotic art, male or female, the site is well worth a visit.

SPECIAL FEATURES

A neatly-animated jumpstation directs surfers to four main choices:

News features information on the artist's work and general information, including a biography, and an interview in Italian. Much of this is accompanied by Manara's artwork, including his interpretation of the story Asion d'Oro and some unpublished sketches of a new character. Both are typical Manara, conveying a deeply erotic feel even with the softest content.

Exhibition featured two sets of Manara artwork when we visited. Sailing Fellini covered 18 drawings dedicated to the Italian director's movies. Kama Sutra showed images from Manara's illustrated Kama Sutra, a beautifully drawn series of couples in various positions.

Things includes books and a CD ROM of Manara's illustrated stories, which are available for ordering online.

Workshop is a small showcase for other artists, of whom three were represented when we visited.

OTHER FEATURES

The site can be emailed, and a number of links are provided.

The official site of a top erotic artist.

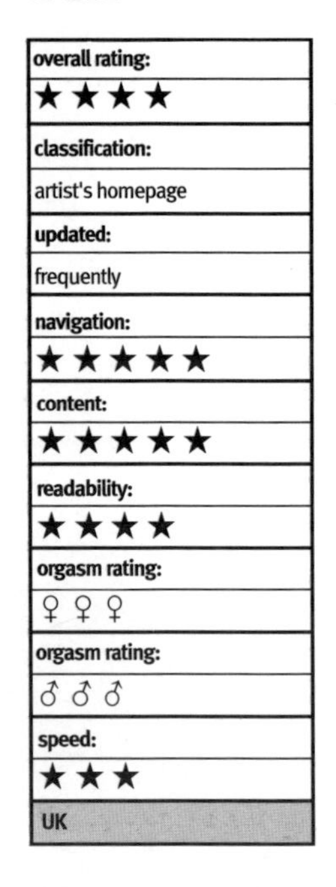

overall rating:
★★★★
classification:
artist's homepage
updated:
frequently
navigation:
★★★★★
content:
★★★★★
readability:
★★★★
orgasm rating:
♀♀♀
orgasm rating:
♂♂♂
speed:
★★★
UK

http://www.wildatheart.co.uk/vinceray.htm

The Vince Ray Experience

This is the website of one of the UK's best known female domination artists. Vince Ray combines a skilled cartoon art style with a sense of humour that anyone not into female domination would probably consider twisted. We loved it, and the whole site, our only complaint being that there could be a great deal more. The design is good and navigation easy, if the bulk of some pages makes it a little slow. It is also entirely free, and is refreshingly short of advertising banners.

SPECIAL FEATURES

Comics features a serialised Vince Ray story, titled Hillybilly Hellcats, which has been lovingly drawn in large format over 11 pages. It takes a while to load but is worth it. The story combines American kitsch with fem dom sex, which is typical of the Vince Ray style. This is set for regular updating, and the site is worth bookmarking just for this feature.

Tattoos gives you a chance to purchase sheets of Vince Ray art as transferable tattoos. These are mainly pieces of classic fem dom imagery, and would add a real touch of attitude to any girl's clubbing look. A sheet of transfers and a tattoo kit cost £14.

Cards Stylish Vince Ray greetings and birthday cards in two styles, 1950s kitsch and elegant oriental, at £2.30 a card or £10 for a set of six.

Mugs Coffee mugs decorated with a large range of Vince Ray artwork. £9 each.

OTHER FEATURES

The price list and order form are in a separate section. Prices are slightly higher outside the UK.

Show site and shop for a leading female domination artist.

overall rating:
★★★
classification:
artist's homepage
updated:
occasionally
navigation:
★★★★
content:
★★★
readability:
★★★★
orgasm rating:
♀♀♀
orgasm rating:
♂♂♂
speed:
★★★★
US

http://sorayama.net

Sorayama Official Website

Hajime Sorayama is arguably the world's foremost erotic artist, creating beautifully-rendered and exotic female figures, perhaps best known from Penthouse magazine. No web guide to erotica would be complete without a review of his work. Sorayama's art is widespread on the net, and often presented in large galleries on both free and paysites, but this site is the official home for his art and so we chose it over the others. Essentially, it is a shop front for his work and is designed to produce sales rather than for the satisfaction of the surfer. Several pieces of art are shown, but at little more than thumbnail size and unexpandable. Nevertheless, the site is free, sufficiently fast and navigable, and provides a useful introduction to the artist.

SPECIAL FEATURES

Art Categories Four of these are offered, each of which leads to a set of small pictures and some information on the art and its background. The categories are Robot, Pinup, Gynoids, and Erotic, covering Sorayama's specialities. The art is beautiful, detailed, imaginative, evocative, and always conveys a sense of the erotic, from the subtle to the powerful. Sadly, the effect is spoiled by the small size of the pictures. Given how widely available Sorayama's art is on the web, albeit regardless of copyright, we felt that not presenting a proper gallery was a pointless and negative exercise.

Sales Books, CD ROMs, Model Kits, T-Shirts, and Art are all offered for sale. The books are impressive, with five albums of Sorayama art offered, ranging in price from $15.95 to $55. No hint is given of what each contains, except in terms of numbers of drawings, which vary from 32 in postcard format to 480 across the artist's full history, from 1964 onwards. The art section offers Sorayama artwork for direct sale. We also looked at the CD ROMs, of which there are two, each with around 125 images, and at t-shirts of which there is a choice of three at $16 per shirt, each printed with a mildly erotic Sorayama image.

OTHER FEATURES

The site also offers an introduction page, a What's New feature, ordering details, and a lengthy Sorayama biography.

A promotional site for perhaps the finest of all erotic artists.

Section 04

for women

Sex sites aimed at women are rare in comparison with those aimed at men, but there are still plenty of them. The majority present galleries of naked men in much the same way as male-orientated sex sites present galleries of women, only instead of Miss All-American Cheerleader you get Mr All-American Jock. Some are more original and we have tried to review a broad selection. Annoying paysites and scams are rarer with porn for women, but surfers should still proceed with caution.

It is received wisdom that men like pictures and women like stories, but this sounded a bit simplistic to us so we did our own survey. The main result (surprise surprise!) was that women, and men, are individuals and different people like different things. In general terms, men seem to prefer plainer, more direct imagery than women, be it as simple as a bare bottom or as apparently obscure as a big toe or even a balloon!

The favourite of most of the women we surveyed was for an image or story that sparks a pet fantasy, such as having a male slave or being spanked. Images of other women and couples in fantasy situations were popular, simple images of naked men remarkably unpopular. We have tried to reflect these findings in the sites we have chosen to review.

One thing we did notice is that women's sites run by women often warn men off, while women's sites run by men often warn gay men off, particularly when nude pictures of the host are on show. In both cases we could think of no better way to ensure that whoever has been warned off does come into the site!

overall rating:
★★★★★
classification:
ezine
updated:
weekly
navigation:
★★★★
content:
★★★★★
readability:
★★★★
orgasm rating:
♀♀♀♀♀
orgasm rating:
♂♂♂
speed:
★★★★
US

www.cleansheets.com

Clean Sheets

If you're aroused by the suggestion of sex, rather than vivid depictions of the sex act, then this could be the site for you. Clean Sheets is a high-quality erotic magazine, with sections on erotic art, features, and fiction.

Throughout the site, the tone of the writing is intelligent and classy. It varies from being subtle to the point of esoteric, to very explicit, though never crude. The various writers all explore different themes and have very different writing styles, but most manage to skillfully describe the subtle nuances of emotion and the frisson leading up to sex, especially at the boundaries where emotion and love blend and give way to sexual excitement.

SPECIAL FEATURES

Fiction is a substantial collection of erotic stories. The writing here acts as a gateway to a fantasy, leaving enough avenues for the reader to explore and expand upon. A common theme through many stories is that of female respect and empowerment, and they are a useful platform for fantasy, for those who want to explore sex within the context of love.

Articles Personal essays on all aspects of sex, from sexual politics to erotic food habits.

Gallery Collection of photographs and paintings by contemporary artists, exploring sexuality and capturing the emotional pleasure and pain manifested by sex.

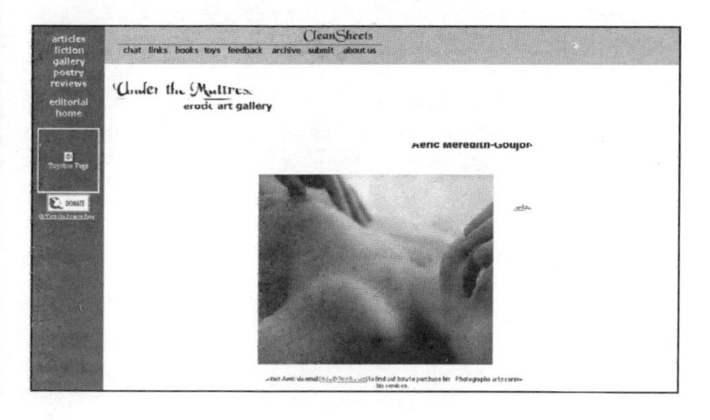

Links There is an extensive list of links to other websites, vetted for quality by Clean Sheets, to reflect their own ethos.

OTHER FEATURES

Books, Feedback and Toys (online shopping), plus a forthcoming Chat section.

High-quality erotic writing for women.

overall rating:
★★★★★
classification:
information
updated:
monthly
navigation:
★★★★
content:
★★★★★
readability:
★★★★★
orgasm rating:
not applicable
orgasm rating:
not applicable
speed:
★★★★
US

www.thriveonline.com/sex/orgasm

The Guide to Women's Orgasm

There is a suprising dearth of sex sites for women on the web, especially ones covering as fundamental a concept as the female orgasm. This site goes some way to filling that gap. At first glance it appears to be rather clinical, but read on – the language used is friendly, down to earth and very clear. All aspects of the female orgasm are covered, from finding your g-spot to female ejaculation, in terms that range from biological to the sensual, on a level that is suitable for even the completely uninitiated. The homepage is simple, with a series of pink buttons down the left-hand side, leading to the different sections of the site. A column of text hyperlinks down the centre of the page lead to the messageboards and advice section with Delilah.

SPECIAL FEATURES

What is an Orgasm? An introduction to how your body reacts during orgasm, and the range of sensations and emotions it may produce.

Vaginal vs Clitoral is a basic introduction of these two areas: including where they are and how to stimulate them. As with any discussion of sex, the variation is endless, but this section sticks to the basic facts and key points for discussion.

Overcoming Difficulties dispels some of the myths and fears that surround the female sexual experience, and prevent women from reaching orgasm.

Multiple Orgasms covers what they are, how they feel, how they happen and most importantly how to feel comfortable with your body's response, whatever the response.

Delilah on Orgasms Resident sexpert, Delilah, answers questions on sex and orgasms, in a forthright but sensitive manner. The range of issues surrounding orgasm is much more complex than simply not being able to have one, and Delilah manages to skillfully negotiate all angles; from feeling at ease with your body's responses, to the politics which can permeate through a relationship and affect sex.

Talk About It is the site's messageboard. Contributions are sincere and are generally of a high standard, focussing on the discussion of sex, rather than flirting with sexual chat.

The G-spot explains the facts and destroys the fiction surrounding this small area of tissue, which has achieved an almost mythical status amongst those searching for it.

OTHER FEATURES

Faking Orgasm, Info for Partners, Ask our Expert.

A good factual start for both males and females wanting to explore the mysteries of the female orgasm.

overall rating:
★★★★
classification:
ezine
updated:
monthly
navigation:
★★★★★
content:
★★★★
readability:
★★★★
orgasm rating:
♀♀♀♀
orgasm rating:
♂♂♂
speed:
★★★★★
US

http://www.eroticaforher.com

Erotica for Her

Erotica for Her is a free ezine celebrating women's sexuality and erotica. It is a large site with plenty of content, which though aimed at women is not anti-male. Despite the size, the site is fast. The layout is good and easy to follow, with a jumpstation on the mainpage, simple text links, and few banners. The style is friendly and fun, with an emphasis on sensual aspects of sex and a touch of the esoteric, but nothing really kinky. While mainly for straight women, we can imagine just about anyone enjoying their visit, with the possible exception of fetishists.

SPECIAL FEATURES

Erotica for Her has numerous features. In addition to monthly articles, it regularly includes: Personals, Shopping, Horoscopes, Zodiac Romance, E-cards, Adult Chat, Sexy Stories, Adult Humor, Sensual Poetry, Galleries, and New from Zecrets.

Articles covers a broad range of sex-related topics. Twelve were online when we visited, from simple advice on women's links to an in-depth piece on the symbolism and significance of coloured and scented candles. We looked at the article on aromatherapeutic massage, which was helpful, and well informed.

Sexy Stories included plenty of choice, with short stories from both men and women. Four new stories had been added in the month we visited. We had a look at Spice and Honeymoon, both pretty straightforward sex stories in a typical US style.

Galleries included 35 thumbnailed galleries. These were mainly of men, but included couples and women. There was a little bondage and a vintage gallery. We looked at Man of the Month Mark, a powerfully-built, long-haired musician pictured stripping and posing. The gallery also gave his email address. Several of the galleries were sponsored by other sites.

Adult Humor included a list of useless sex facts such as the average length of an erect penis being 5.1 inches (we wondered what figure you'd get if you asked instead of actually measured!). Not all the facts are so useless; apparently men's sperm tastes nice and sweet if they've been eating acidic fruit such as oranges and kiwi, but disgusting after asparagus.

New from Zecrets provides erotic pictures of men and couples, including hardcore, and is sponsored by the Erotica for Women site Zecrets.com.

OTHER FEATURES

The site also provides links, and is illustrated with pictures and quotes.

A great erotic ezine if perhaps a little straight for some. Designed for women but worthwhile for all.

overall rating:
★★★★
classification:
homepage
updated:
occasionally
navigation:
★★★★
content:
★★★
readability:
★★★★
orgasm rating:
♀♀♀
orgasm rating:
♂♂♂
speed:
★★★
US

http://www.knottymoon.com

Knottymoon's Spanking Haven for Women

Knottymoon's is a personal take on spanking, with a firmly female viewpoint. Men are discouraged, and submissive men directed to her female domination area, although the site is actually nearly as much fun for male spanking enthusiasts as for females. It will also be reassuring for inexperienced dominant males to see a genuine, free site by a woman who loves both spanking and being spanked. The style is light-hearted and enthusiastic. Advertising is kept to a minimum on principal, and the mainpage has a useful summary of the traps and irritations that she dislikes. Although the site is a little wordy and cluttered, the design is generally good. The only criticism was that there could have been much more material.

SPECIAL FEATURES

Stories features a few on-site stories, with more links to other spanking story sites and recommended books. We looked at My Spanking Travels with a Male Sub, which was fun, and had the genuine feel that makes the site worthwhile.

Forum A women's forum for discussion of spanking and spanking-related matters. This had plenty of messages when we visited, many with discussions, all of which are text-linked from the entry page. These covered a variety of topics, including reminiscences of genuine spanking experiences (well, hopefully). We took a look at a rather nice one from a girl who had been spanked at a party after losing a bet, which had the right feel, genuine or not. The forum is policed and inappropriate messages deleted.

Spanking Art covers a series of small galleries showing mainly female submissive spanking art. This is a nice selection, and most pictures bring the feel of the fantasy across well enough, though given the amount of spanking art around we felt that a few more wouldn't have hurt. Below the galleries a selection of spanking art sites are reviewed, most of which need AVS.

OTHER FEATURES

Extensive links are offered in several categories, and in many cases reviewed, both for spanking and general erotica. The Altavista translation service is linked. The site is a member of several webrings.

A woman's personal take on spanking fantasy.

overall rating:	★★★★
classification:	listings
updated:	frequently
navigation:	★★★★
content:	★★★★
readability:	★★★★
orgasm rating:	not applicable
orgasm rating:	not applicable
speed:	★★★
US	

http://www.ladylynx.com

Lady Lynx

Lady Lynx is a listings site for adult sites specifically designed for women. By this they mean women who are into men, as there is very little content that would interest lesbians, although gay men might well enjoy a peep at the gallery listings. The site is easy to navigate if a little slow, and while there are advertising banners, these are not particularly obtrusive. We enjoyed our visit, but felt the content could have been a little broader. The link on the mainpage that male visitors are supposed to follow simply leads to a short list of paysites, although we couldn't think of a more effective way to ensure that men visit the site than suggesting that they go away.

SPECIAL FEATURES

Lady Lynx divides listings into seven categories. Each link is given with a brief review of the content, the date it was added, and the number of hits generated.

Erotic Stories had 59 links when we visited, including general story sites and individual women's homepages, with poetry as well as fiction and some factual pieces. General sites with an emphasis on stories are also included.

Fetish included 28 links, which are not necessarily women's sites, but which reflect popular female fantasies, in particular being on the receiving end of spankings and domination.

Galleries covered 77 sites. Most of these featured naked men, although there were a fair selection of couples and also some artwork sites. Styles vary, but the content is in the main straight.

Link Lists had 32 other listing sites, emphasising those with a 'for women' slant, but including many more general ones.

Miscellaneous contained 27 links. Some were unusual, such as Real Women don't do Housework, while others were more general (although many of them seemed to belong in the other categories).

Pay and AVS features 40 links to major women-oriented paysites.

Products/Services Seventy-one links to shops. Many sound worthwhile, but they are only of use if you can order from the US with a credit card.

OTHER FEATURES

The site also offers shopping and a mailing list for updates.

A good listings site for women's erotica.

overall rating:
★★★★
classification:
homepage
updated:
monthly
navigation:
★★★★
content:
★★★★
readability:
★★★★★
orgasm rating:
♀♀♀♀
orgasm rating:
♂♂♂♂
speed:
★★★
US

http://www.catacomb.sexplanets.com/nowhere

Nowhere Girl

Nowhere Girl is a gallery site for lovers of erotic gothic imagery. The hostess is Dee, who signs herself Nowhere Girl. It took a while to get into the site, with two preliminary pages, but inside the design is good and simple. There are banner ads, but as she points out, these are placed there by the hosting company. The style is honest and humorous, and we enjoyed reading the text areas as much as visiting the galleries. While not intended specifically for women, the site has a sensual, feminine feel to it.

SPECIAL FEATURES

Welcome is the introduction, where Dee explains how she feels that most of the porn sites on the net are designed for football fans who like cheerleaders with dyed blonde hair and fake breasts. As a result, she intends to provide something different. This she describes as, 'girls who are made of Spiders and Lace and Cobwebs drawn on the face, Chains and Whips and Metal Hoops.'

FAQ provides answers to questions, mainly anticipating criticism of the site. For instance, why there are only females in the galleries. The answer? She likes girls, and why not?

Galleries is the main feature of the site. When we visited there were seven quite large galleries. These change regularly, but when we visited they included a two-gallery sequence of two girls making love in a cemetery, and five themed galleries of individual goth girls. We visited the cemetery sequence, which was perhaps a little too posed but very sensual, with 48 pictures, from the girl entering the cemetery fully-clothed to huddled naked on the steps of a mausoleum. Emily in White showed 20 pictures of a girl playing with a pair of handcuffs on a bed, with every detail being white except for the cuffs and her stockings. Again, this was sensual, uninhibited, and could well be fantasy-provoking; yet obviously it won't be to everyone's taste. All pictures are thumbnailed and big enough to see what's going on before clicking for the larger version.

OTHER FEATURES

Nowhere Girl provides links to related sites, news, a guestbook, and plenty of comment.

A goth girl's gallery site, dark and sensual.

overall rating:
★★★★
classification:
free erotica
updated:
monthly
navigation:
★★★★
content:
★★★★
readability:
★★★★★
orgasm rating:
♀♀♀♀
orgasm rating:
♂
speed:
★★★★★
US

http://www.nerve.com

Nerve.com

Nerve.com is an online version of the US-based print magazine, and describes itself as a 'smart, honest magazine on sex'. In fact, this is selling themselves short since it's much more than a magazine on sex: it's a lifestyle magazine, with sex as a starting point. The homepage looks overcrowded, but to find the section you want simply scroll down the page and click on the titles in the central column.

SPECIAL FEATURES

The Regulars A broad spectrum of topical news and features, including The Diaries of Lisa Carver, This Week in Sex (sex-related news from around the world), and even a feature on sexual reproduction and genetics.

Personal Essays Real-life contributions on sexual experiences, including 'Celebrity First Times'.

Fiction Stories which are more forthright than a lot of other erotic writing aimed at women, but more gentle than porn.

Nervecenter The interactive hub of the site, where you can participate in a daily poll, indulge in live chat, or check out the personal ads.

Packed magazine surpasses its aim of being a fearless, intelligent forum on sex.

http://pcforwomen.com

Planet Cock for Women

Planet Cock for Women is a free site dedicated to women's erotica. The format is that of an ezine, with features other than straightforward erotica. Unfortunately, the framed jumpstation and the mainpage jumpstation did not have the same content when we visited, which made it a little confusing. The style is open and lustful, although the content is strictly solo men only, with no couples or sex acts, but plenty of erect penises.

overall rating:
★★★★
classification:
free erotica
updated:
monthly
navigation:
★★★★
content:
★★★★
readability:
★★★★★
orgasm rating:
♀♀♀♀
orgasm rating:
♂
speed:
★★★★★
US

SPECIAL FEATURES

What's On is a mainpage feature for updates, comment and feedback.

Galleries is the main feature of the site, with several large thumbnailed galleries of naked men. The galleries are divided into semi-naked, naked, and amateurs, along with Furry Men and Hot Cocks. The emphasis is on powerfully-built, muscular young men.

Ask a Dick is a Q&A feature where women ask a man sex-related questions. The answers were frank, but rather innocent.

Just for Fun is a collection of witty remarks and jokes at the expense of men.

A well-presented, useful site for straight women, with plenty of pictures of men.

overall rating:
★★★★
classification:
erotic ezine
updated:
monthly
navigation:
★★★★
content:
★★★★
readability:
★★★
orgasm rating:
♀♀♀♀
orgasm rating:
♂♂♂
speed:
★★★
US

http://www.sexythinking.com

Sexy Thinking

Sexy Thinking is an erotic ezine for women, by women. The site presents a broad range of erotica, which is subtle but not necessarily soft. There are many contributors, male as well as female, thus providing variety. In style it is open, friendly, and certainly feminine. The design is good, with a jumpstation at the top of each page for easy navigation, and clear text or thumbnailed links. Unfortunately, this is spoilt by an excess of banners, which are mainly for paysites and include some designed to be misleading.

SPECIAL FEATURES

Photos consists of 16 galleries, of approximately 12 pictures each. These are mostly designed to be provocative rather than blatantly sexual, but that does not necessarily mean they are softcore. Men are also featured, but the majority are of women. Many are in galleries by specific photographers. We especially enjoyed Dany Nieves's picture of a black woman seated naked on the loo with a magazine, which manages to be deliciously naughty yet also innocent.

Stories is a good-sized collection of erotic short stories broken down into categories: Mariana 's Favourites, Exotic Fiction, Love Stories, Hardcore Tales, and BDSM. We looked at Exotic Fiction, which covers unusual erotic fantasy stories and so on. The stories show more imagination and skill than many on the net.

However, most have a distinctly American flavour which UK readers may not enjoy.

Art Erotica from a number of featured artists. We looked at John Squadra, who produces sensual, sometimes abstract images with great skill.

Poetry is a collection of gently erotic poems. We enjoyed these and felt they could certainly be arousing in the right context.

Amateurs features girls from Amateurpages.com, so this is essentially an advert.

Reviews When we visited, a single review was posted of the erotic novel A Dot on the Map by David O. Dyer Sr.

OTHER FEATURES

The site has no links section as such, and most of the links on the pages are to paysites. When we visited, the XXX section only led back to the main page, while another promised link took us to Kara's Adult Playground: a good paysite, but still a paysite.

An excellent erotic ezine for women slightly spoilt by advertising.

overall rating:
★★★★
classification:
erotica
updated:
monthly
navigation:
★★★★
content:
★★★★
readability:
★★★
orgasm rating:
♀♀♀♀
orgasm rating:
♂♂♂
speed:
★★★★
US

http://www.venusorvixen.com

Venus or Vixen

Venus or Vixen is a site run by a group of women to promote literary erotica and erotic photography. The main page tells surfers to read some smut, which has to be good advice, and gives an idea of what the site is all about. The site is presented in frames, with several irritating banners that reduce the readability. Other than that, there is a jumpstation for ease of navigation, and behind the banners the design is good. The style is friendly, open, and positive, presenting erotica as a pleasure without guilt.

SPECIAL FEATURES

Erotica covers short stories submitted to VOV. Four were accessible from text links when we visited, while another link led to the archives. Stories may also be commented on and your own stories submitted. We looked at The Newsroom by Cassandra Snow, which is well written and uninhibited, although perhaps rather florid at times. In this case the sex is very straightforward.

Art Venus or Vixen features an erotic artist each month. When we visited, links to the last four months' artists were available. We looked at Tattooed by David Naz, a collection of mildly erotic and atmospheric works relating to tattoos, presented one at a time. Other art features included Nudes Masked, looking at the erotic appeal derived from combining nudity with a masked face.

Viscera is the latest title from VOV. This is a collection of 18 erotic short stories edited by Cara Bruce. The content varies, but it does include some powerful erotica and exotic fantasies, many of which play with the boundaries of what is and is not taboo. This has been well reviewed, including some positive comments by Kathleen Bryson of Virgin Publishing on this side of the Atlantic, and is available from Amazon.

About Us gives biographies of the staff at VOV. Four of the five people involved are women, including Cara Bruce, the editor, who is also a well established writer of erotic fiction in the US.

OTHER FEATURES

Venus or Vixen also presents archives, features, columns, reviews, and a serial. A shop and press feedback page are promised for the future.

A good literary erotica site with erotic photography as well.

Section 05

man to man

While the sites in this chapter have been created very much with men identifying as gay in mind, we are aware that the chapter itself is in no way exhaustive or comprehensive. Gay male sex, in all its variations, has a strong presence on the net, and to do it full justice requires a separate Good Web Guide (which is due for publication in 2001).

This chapter, then, is essentially for the bi-curious: men with a latent or burgeoning interest in sex with other men, or those who just plain old want to know what two men get up to in bed!

http://www.bearhug.net

BearHug

BearHug's Homepage is the site for a gay men's social group with an interest in bears (hairy men that is, not the sort of bear you get in the wild). This is a London-based club, but with a national membership. The site is colourful, with a friendly, easy-going style. It is reasonably fast, and the main page includes an introduction to the club, updates, and contact points, making for quick access. The site is entirely free, with no banners or other irritations. The site is an ideal resource for this social group.

overall rating:
★★★★★
classification:
club
updated:
frequently
navigation:
★★★★★
content:
★★★★★
readability:
★★★★★
orgasm rating:
♀
orgasm rating:
♂♂♂
speed:
★★★★
UK

SPECIAL FEATURES

Link of the Month This is a feature to promote related sites, in this case bear-ware.com, a site offering commercial artwork on the bear theme.

Information covers the club and the ideas behind it. Essentially, it is a social club designed for gay men who are either big and hairy or have a preference for big, hairy men. The emphasis is on friendliness and a relaxed atmosphere. There is no dress code, and they stress that the club is for older men as well as the young, single, gay males who tend to dominate the gay scene.

Events are set out month by month and cover both club events and more general gay events. When we visited, the London Mardi Gras 2000 was listed, along with a BearHug bowling event, and visits to the Millennium Wheel, a club, and a sauna.

The majority of these events are London-based, although BearHug is keen to take on a more national identity and in the past has included Manchester, Rugby, and Brighton.

Venues Bear-friendly venues around the country.

Gallery is the BearHug picture collection, and not an erotic gallery, showing photos from BearHug events. When we visited, there were individual galleries from 18 events, and the overall impression was of a very friendly, broad-based social group.

Links includes direct links to several members' homepages.

OTHER FEATURES

General links to related sites are also listed, and BearHug is a member of the Bear Ring.

A social group for hairy, gay men and their admirers. Also a useful resource and starting point.

http://www.g-l-n.co.uk

Gay London News

Gay London News is a truly impressive resource for gay London. The listings are extensive, along with news, links, and shopping; just about everything except galleries, of which they feel there are enough elsewhere. Navigation is easy, with a system of jumpstations to guide you around the site, although the sheer volume of information presented can make it slow going, while much of the text is in small fonts. There are no banners and few pictures, making the site much faster than it would otherwise be. Personal ads can be placed for free in all relevant areas, with low charges for the inclusion of photos.

overall rating:
★★★★★
classification:
ezine
updated:
daily
navigation:
★★★★
content:
★★★★★
readability:
★★★
orgasm rating:
not applicable
orgasm rating:
not applicable
speed:
★★★★★
UK

SPECIAL FEATURES

The main page of GLN is in frames, containing news and listing 13 principal subsections. These are: Listings, Resources, The Forum, Contacts, Market Place, Shopping, Downloads, Fun, Contact Us, Tourist Info, Links, What's New, and Awards.

Resources covers Accommodation, Campaigning Groups, Clubs and Groups, Sexual Health, Publications, and Services for gay men. These are defined as those operating primarily in the London area.

Listings is the heart of the site, with gay locations and events of all sorts listed both by area and on a day-to-day basis. This covers a great deal of information, and a cross-referencing system is due to be introduced to make it even more efficient.

Some events are covered in more detail on the main page.

We also had a look at the GLN Market Place, which allows text-only adverts to be placed free of charge by anyone who wishes to buy, sell, or swap anything worldwide. Businesses may advertise at £15 for six months or £20 for a year, which includes a picture. Downloads allows surfers to obtain useful programs, of which there are five at present, including Cu-SeeMe and IRC software. Shopping includes a deal with Amazon UK for access to books, music, videos and DVDs, many at cut prices. The Forum allows visitors to the site to leave messages and keep in touch, for free. Their Contacts section is also free and worldwide for anyone interested in meeting gay men from London.

OTHER FEATURES

The site also contains numerous snippets of information, and presents awards to other quality gay sites.

An excellent, London-based gay resource.

http://www.allruggedmen.com

All Rugged Men

All Rugged Men is a gay gallery site dedicated to pictures of men naked in the great outdoors. As they say, these are the sort of men who wear hiking boots all the time and take you skinny-dipping in a river on a date, followed, no doubt by a barbecue over an open fire. The site is large and easy enough to navigate, although there are quite a few advertising banners, including ones for straight-sex paysites.

overall rating:
★★★★
classification:
gallery
updated:
occasionally
navigation:
★★★★
content:
★★★★
readability:
★★★
orgasm rating:
♀♀♀
orgasm rating:
♂♂♂♂
speed:
★★★★
US

SPECIAL FEATURES

The site contains 13 galleries, each with around 15 images. Each gallery is of one individual pictured in a series of outdoor poses. These are softcore, with no sex acts shown, and the majority of models clothed or partially clothed. Each gallery is a set of thumbnails, which in turn lead to good-sized, clear pictures. While not a site for those craving full-on pictures of gay sex, the imagery is good, with the emphasis on a hardy, muscular look. The models are not named though, which made it seem rather impersonal. The first one we looked at showed a handsome young man in a cornfield, with his jeans on and in poses that would pass unnoticed in a public park. The second was a little harder, showing an older, beefier man stripping nude against a backdrop of fields and woods. Taken outside the gay context, these images may be as likely to appeal to women as men.

OTHER FEATURES

Other than links to paysites, All Rugged Men contains no additional features.

A good free site for softcore gay galleries featuring men outdoors.

http://www.freegaypix.com

Free Gay Pictures

overall rating:
★★★★
classification:
gallery
updated:
weekly
navigation:
★★★★
content:
★★★★★
readability:
★★★
orgasm rating:
♀♀
orgasm rating:
♂♂♂♂
speed:
★★★★
US

Free Gay Pictures is a large gay men's gallery site boasting over 2,000 pictures. These vary from softcore to hardcore, but are mainstream, with nothing kinky; they are what might be termed gay vanilla. The site is a straightforward gallery site; simple and fast, but slowed by banners advertising those gay paysites that sponsor the site. When we visited there was also one advertising pop-up, which we found more irritating than any number of banners. Despite the banners, the navigation was easy and effective, with links from pictures that made it very clear what you could expect to get. The style is a little neutral, although for those after plenty of rude gay pictures and nothing more the site cannot be faulted.

SPECIAL FEATURES

The galleries are divided into 12 categories: 3ways/Group, Anal Action, Cum Shots, Series, Sucking, Non-Nude, Black Studs, Nude, Rimming/Ass Licking, Uniforms, Asians, and Uncut. Most of these are self-explanatory. Uncut is for those who enjoy pictures of intact foreskins. These galleries are accessed from a big pictoral jumpstation. Click on your choice and you go to a page listing the galleries within that category, as well as several advertising banners. Chose a gallery and you go to a page with more advertising and a thumbnail gallery with 30 or so pictures. Each of these thumbnails goes in turn to a large, high resolution picture of your choice. We chose Black Studs, then gallery No 4, which contained 30 pictures of well-muscled black men either alone or having sex. Inevitably, there is some overlap in the categories between galleries, but we thought there ought to be enough here to keep the most avid gay porn fanatic happy as long as he's not looking for anything kinky.

OTHER FEATURES

The site also gives you a chance to vote for your favourite gallery to be updated. All links are to sponsoring paysites, including some that are designed to be deliberately misleading.

A pretty comprehensive gallery site for mainstream gay sex.

http://www.gaydar.co.uk

Gaydar

Gaydar is a free UK-based gay men's resource site. Although not strictly a contact site, the focus is on communication. The site is in frames, fast and easy to navigate, with a simple, honest style and no distractions. The mainpage gives direct links to some areas and a detailed jumpstation. While not a sex site as such, Gaydar has a clear erotic slant and a little soft gay erotic content.

overall rating:
★★★★
classification:
specialist service
updated:
frequently
navigation:
★★★★★
content:
★★★★
readability:
★★★★★
orgasm rating:
♀
orgasm rating:
♂♂♂
speed:
★★★★
UK

SPECIAL FEATURES

Gaydar is divided into four principal sections: Communicate, News, Shop and Sell, and Other. Site registration may be completed from the Mainpage and is free.

Communicate covers the Gaydar personals, ecards, chat, and netmeeting (see Interactive). Ecards allows surfers to send electronic greetings cards from three categories: humorous, cityscapes, and men, which is a range of gay erotic art photos. Chat gives access to the site chatroom, and netmeeting to a list of gay men's webcams, including information as to who is online at any given time. There was plenty of choice when we visited, including bisexuals and a 'watersports' enthusiast. Email addresses are also provided. Personals also provided a good list of offers, though not necessarily all within the UK.

Shop and Sell covers Shopping, Classifieds, Links, and Bookwise. These are by no means all related to erotica, but to gay issues in general. Shopping covers a range of products, which are gay-specific but not actual sex aids. These can be purchased with a shopping-cart system. We looked at Wacky Weenies, a range of novelty dildos designed as presents rather than for actual insertion (or so we hope, looking at the Elephant Penis and Lick the Lizard!). Classifieds covers areas such as accommodation and employment, and is distinct from the personals section. Links included 13 adult sites, many of which were clubs and professional services. Bookwise offers a selection of books, which again are generally gay rather than specifically erotic. Having selected a category, you are taken to a list of books, each with a synopsis. Gay Fantasy contained five titles when we visited, including historic and science-fiction fantasies.

OTHER FEATURES

Gaydar's news feature covers gay lifestyle with a UK emphasis. Site policy and contact are given in the Other section.

A useful resource for the UK gay community with an emphasis on contact.

http://www.gummi.org.uk

Gummi

Gummi is a club set up exclusively for gay men who are into rubber. This is specialist, no doubt, but also distinctive, covering a popular area of fetishism that in turn leads to other, yet more specialist areas. While some of the rubberwear featured is very stylish, Gummi is not intended simply as a rubber fashion club. The website is small and straightforward, readable and easy to navigate, but slower than it might be. The style is open and enthusiastically devoted to rubber and rubbery sexual behaviour, although there is little erotic content. There are no banners or distractions, and several rubbery artwork illustrations for decoration.

Note: these guys are experts. Before you play rubber enclosure games, make sure you know exactly what you are doing.

overall rating:
★★★★
classification:
club
updated:
frequently
navigation:
★★★★
content:
★★★★
readability:
★★★★★
orgasm rating:
♀
orgasm rating:
♂♂♂
speed:
★★★
UK

SPECIAL FEATURES

Next Events is the list of up-coming Gummi events. These occur once a month at Central Station near King's Cross. A link is provided to access a map for anyone who doesn't know this famous gay hangout. When we visited, two events were advertised, each with a theme. The themes were Mask, Hoods and Gags, and Harnesses, all in rubber of course.

How to Join gives membership details for the club. As a group of genuine enthusiasts rather than a money-making scheme, Gummi is cheap at only £10 a year. For this, members receive low admission rates to events, although the actual ticket prices were not given. There is also a chance to win prizes in a monthly raffle, discounting at various rubberwear suppliers, advance booking for tickets to events, and a bimonthly Rubber Sheet (their newsletter). This represents pretty good value.

Rubber Links contains not merely links to like-minded sites such as the wonderfully-named US club Sludgemaster, but also to suppliers of heavy duty protective clothing and marine gear.

Photos is a page of photos from Gummi events, some of which link on to further small galleries. These include mud-wrestling in rubber, being encased in tyres, and rubbery mummification.

Rear of the Year Male buttocks encased in tight black rubber, anyone?

OTHER FEATURES

Gummi can be contacted by email, and their postal address is also given.

A club site for gay men into rubber.

http://www.smgays.org

SMGays

SM Gays is a non-profit-making social and educational group for gay men interested in consensual, sexual sadomasochism. Founded in 1981, they now play an important part in the UK's gay SM community, and also support the SM community in general. The site is small, free, and intended as an information resource to encourage safe and lawful SM practices and to provide understanding of their often criticised field of sexual interest. The site is fast, simple, readable, and easy to navigate, although there could have been more content, even for a voluntary group. In style it is perhaps a little stern.

overall rating:
★★★★
classification:
specialist service
updated:
frequently
navigation:
★★★★★
content:
★★★★
readability:
★★★★★
orgasm rating:
♀
orgasm rating:
♂♂♂
speed:
★★★★★
UK

SPECIAL FEATURES

The main SM Gays page covers three principal areas, each accessible from a jumpstation at the top of the page. Each area then links to further information.

Activities A regular calendar of events is posted. Meetings are at the Hoist Club in Vauxhall and take place on the third Thursday of each month. Each meeting has an educational theme related to the world of gay SM sex. When we visited, the subjects coming up were Cock and Ball Treatments, Chest and Nipple Stimulation, and Hoods and Helmets. A lot of experience goes into these meetings, and it will be very few people indeed who cannot learn something.

Publications When we visited, the group was advertising four books and a number of information sheets. Three of the books were different resource books, and the fourth was Rough Sex Safer Sex, which is also available to read online. This is candidly presented and extremely useful for anybody practising SM sex. Heterosexual SMers will also find much of the information valuable, and we recommend it to anybody interested in exploring this area of sex, especially novices.

Information provides a direct link to Rough Sex Safer Sex and an area on SM and the Law. Finally, a statement is included stressing the group's opposition to sexism, fascism, and racism.

OTHER FEATURES

The SM Gays site is designed specifically to promote their aims. Few links lead from the site, and although the group may be contacted by email, they do not enter into correspondence outside their official events.

A social and support group for gay men involved in SM.

Section 06

woman to woman

Though the emphasis here is on women having sex with women, we do not pretend that those who define themselves as lesbians will find all their net needs met by the selection of sites within. To do justice to the wealth of sites covering all aspects of lesbian sex, a separate book would be necessary.

Woman to Woman is primarily for those who might be termed bi-curious: women interested in exploring the possiblities of sapphic delights and for those who just enjoy the idea of women together, whether they're women themselves or not.

overall rating:	★★★★★
classification:	homepage
updated:	occasionally
navigation:	★★★★
content:	★★★★★
readability:	★★★
orgasm rating:	♀♀♀♀
orgasm rating:	♀♀♀♀
speed:	★★★
US	

http://www.webmistress.org/crave

Crave

This is the free homepage of a submissive lesbian BDSM enthusiast. Not only does she present several galleries on her favourite subject, but also a considerable amount of advice and explanation, which is valuable not only to lesbians but to anyone practising BDSM. Such advice is always best from the viewpoint of an intelligent, informed submissive, and the sincerity and understanding of Crave earns the site five stars. The design is simple and effective, although it is cluttered with advertising banners and not particularly fast. Several sections can be viewed with or without frames. Although a lesbian site, anyone into BDSM is going to get a lot out of a visit.

SPECIAL FEATURES

Explanation consists of several pages explaining the author's ethos and attitude to BDSM. These are intelligent and well written, from a personal perspective. Aside from general information, she provides negotiation forms and a checklist of SM information. She also explains the distinction between SM and abuse.

Music Recommended music for BDSM scenes, in most cases complete with links to the artist's official site. Her selection ranges from obscure lesbian bands to such mainstream artists as Madonna and Peter Gabriel, and shows considerable breadth of personal perspective.

Writing features the author's own erotica, which is very personal and seen from the lesbian submissive viewpoint. This has power and is of a much higher standard than most of the erotic writing on the net. We read Labia Piercing, her description of having her labia pierced by a gay man, which was both detailed and vivid, allowing the reader to experience her feelings as if from inside her head.

Images is a set of nine thumbnailed galleries of women in BDSM situations. These mainly involve bondage, some in posed dungeon situations, and others of a more subtle nature. Some show women together, but the majority show women alone. Our personal favourite was of a girl lying on her front with her hands tied back to her ankles. She has no top on, her jeans have been pulled down and she is smiling happily at the camera. Posed, no doubt, but this encapsulates the feel of Crave.

OTHER FEATURES

Crave also provides extensive links to BDSM related sites of all sorts, although with a US bias.

An excellent lesbian BDSM homepage.

overall rating:
★★★★★
classification:
ezine
updated:
monthly
navigation:
★★★★★
content:
★★★★
readability:
★★★★
orgasm rating:
♀♀♀♀♀
orgasm rating:
♀♀♀
speed:
★★★★
US

http://www.gfriends.com/onourbacks

On Our Backs – The Best of Lesbian Sex

On Our Backs is the resurrected version of the famous lesbian magazine originally edited by Susie Bright. It is now a sister title to Girlfriends Magazine and belongs to HAF Enterprises, but technically it is celebrating its 15th anniversary. The ezine is well designed, highly readable, and easy to navigate, with excellent erotic content that impressed us with both breadth and depth, if not quantity. While a lesbian magazine, it has to be admitted that many men will also enjoy it. Being a West Coast USA publication, it is perhaps not all that it might be for British surfers, but we recommend a visit.

SPECIAL FEATURES

The On Our Backs mainpage gives links to four main areas:

Girls included three photo galleries when we visited. These were small, and black and white, but with excellent content and evocative lesbian imagery, which was sometimes subtle, sometimes strong. We looked at Angel Baby, which showed a girl undressing and peeing on the beach, and Birthday Bang, which showed one girl eating cake from another's body; great stuff! Presumably the hardcopy magazine shows these in their full glory.

Fiction included two erotic short stories when we visited. We tried 'You Want Fries With That?' By Jennifer Hunter, a story about sexy fun in a burger bar. This was messy and fun and quite well written, and for once the US style didn't spoil it for us.

Reality is the section for serious articles, of which there were four. We looked at How to Play with Fire by Deborah Addington. This provides advice on fireplay, one of the most dangerous and tricky of all SM activities. The article is sensible and intelligently written, explaining how to create exquisite sensations without causing damage. Nevertheless, this is definitely not a game for the inexperienced. Other articles included the regular Adventure Girl feature and general advice.

Magazine covers subscription information for the magazine, a T-Shirt offer, and a chance to sign up for a free online newsletter.

OTHER FEATURES

The site also provides links to the archives, which had very little in them at the time of our visit. There is also contact information and information about the magazine.

An excellent lesbian ezine from the US.

overall rating:
★★★★
classification:
ezine
updated:
weekly
navigation:
★★★
content:
★★★★★
readability:
★★★★
orgasm rating:
not applicable
orgasm rating:
not applicable
speed:
★★★★
UK

http://www.dykesnow.com

DykesNow

DykesNow is a UK-based free ezine and resource designed specifically for lesbians. It is new, but full of potential, with an out-and-proud style. It is not intended as an erotica site, but there is an unabashed erotic content. The design is good, with a jumpstation at the top of each page, although we felt that with such an overload of US sites on the net it was a mistake to have a picture of the Statue of Liberty on the mainpage. We also found a few teething problems with the navigation system. There is plenty of content, and when mature, this should be an excellent resource for the lesbian community.

SPECIAL FEATURES

Mainpage Features provides links to news and a number of articles. There is a weekly report from the editor, Claire Benjamin, listings, eating and travel, as well as the main jumpstation. When we visited, articles included something on fashion shoots, shopping at the women-run sex shop Sh!, fitness tips, and information on sex, housing, and money. The galleries are also directly linked from this page.

Listings covers lesbian and lesbian-friendly venues and events. These are broken down by region, covering the whole of mainland Britain.

Homepages DykesNow offers personal homepage space to visitors. When we visited, these were not linked from the site.

Galleries features two galleries, not of models, but of lesbian amateurs having fun. Some are naughty, most are not. Flash is needed to view these, and can be downloaded free from the gallery page.

Links is a main feature of the site and is divided into categories, including sex and erotica links. Music, clubs, social groups, Magazines and Ezines, Design, World, Travel, and Fashion links are covered, although there were rather few when we visited.

OTHER FEATURES

DykesNow also offers webcams, chatrooms, forums, and personals. These are new features and are only just beginning to come to life, so it is impossible to assess them at this stage. The design is good, with each section divided into relevant subsections. The personals will be covered by regions and major cities. Forums are set up for social issues, the scene, and sex. All of this will be entirely free.

A new but fine ezine for the lesbian community.

overall rating:
★★★★
classification:
ezine
updated:
frequently
navigation:
★★★★★
content:
★★★★
readability:
★★★★
orgasm rating:
not applicable
orgasm rating:
not applicable
speed:
★★★
UK

http://dykeuniverse.com

Dyke Universe

Dyke Universe is a resource site, created by women, for women, and is UK-based. The erotic content is minimal, but it is nevertheless a useful lesbian resource. The style is open, humorous, and easy-going. A large jumpstation provides quick access from the mainpage to the rest of the site, and remains as a left-hand column on most other pages. It is perhaps a little cluttered and somewhat slow, but the content is good and well presented, in an ezine style. Although a UK site, Dyke Universe is closely linked to the much larger and more fully developed US lesbian net community, and those seeking UK facilities may often find themselves in US sites.

SPECIAL FEATURES

The Dyke Universe mainpage lists 12 main areas: Dyke Radio, Team, Hot Topics, TV Divas, Agony Aunty, Health, The Rag, Events, Fun Stuff, Film Reviews, Book Reviews, and Poetry. The Team consists of four women; three writers and the Agony Aunty. We visited the Agony Aunty section, which gave eight letter titles as text links to the letters and answers. These dealt mainly with serious lesbian issues, such as the difficulties of coming out and violence within lesbian relationships. The replies are genuine and sympathetic, providing good advice in the face of often intractable problems. Events provided five links, covering the London Mardi Gras 2000 and the dyke scenes in London, Oxford, Bournemouth, and Brighton. These were well researched and informative, if somewhat limited in scope, and we felt a more national approach would be valuable. The London section listed three venues: the Candy Bar Club, Loose, a girly strip joint, and Flirt, a sauna bar, all in central London. Book reviews were again good but limited, covering only three titles, and all of these classics: Joanna Trollope's A Village Affair, Oranges Are Not the Only Fruit by Jeanette Winterson, and Radclyffe Hall's The Well of Lonliness. More content is promised, but the site clearly has to develop to reach its full potential.

OTHER FEATURES

Dyke Universe contains many minor features, extensive links, a message board, a chatroom, a guestbook, news, and comments.

A good, general resource for lesbians.

overall rating:
★★★★
classification:
homepage
updated:
occasionally
navigation:
★★★★★
content:
★★★★
readability:
★★★★★
orgasm rating:
♀♀♀♀
orgasm rating:
♂♂
speed:
★★★
US

http://sappho.com

The Isle of Lesbos

Alexandra North's Isle of Lesbos site clearly states that it is not a sex site and that there are no photographs of nude women. Nevertheless, the content is undoubtedly erotic, at least in part. However, if you want straightforward porn then this is not the site for you. The style is personal, gentle, and intellectual, as well as sensual, and while the content is clearly designed for lesbian surfers, it would be naïve to assume that straight women and men might not also enjoy a visit. It is free and has no banners or other irritations at all. The design is good, while it is easy to navigate and very readable, with a good balance of information and pictures.

SPECIAL FEATURES

About this Site gives you a brief introduction to the site.

Poetry is an impressive catalogue of Lesbian and Bisexual female poets, from Sappho herself to contemporary poets. A short biography of each is given, and in some cases samples of their work.

Classical Art features art relating to lesbian imagery rather than art by lesbians, and is a catalogue covering 40 artists or schools. These can be browsed by artist or time period, and include such classics as The Echo by Jean-François Auburtin, a study of three long-haired, naked girls looking out across a scape of sea and mountains. This is sensual, subtle, and, we felt, erotic.

Vintage Images Postcards and old photographs containing lesbian or lesbian-related imagery. These vary from pictures with no obvious erotic content but which can be interpreted as expressing love between women, to naughty French postcards.

Letters and Journals Published excerpts from the private letters and journals of various notable women, including Vita Sackville-West and Emily Dickinson.

Web Directory Extensive, categorised links covering a lesbian outlook on art, literature, business, health, and more.

Quotations is a collection of remarks by or about lesbians. Our favourite sums up what we feel should be the best attitude to erotica: 'Why should I paint dead fish, onions, and beer glasses? Girls are so much prettier.' (Marie Laurencin, artist)

OTHER FEATURES

In addition to the Web Directory, a few other links are included on individual pages. The site may also be emailed.

A fine resource site for lesbian art and culture, both erotic and romantic.

overall rating:
★★★
classification:
homepage
updated:
occasionally
navigation:
★★★
content:
★★★★
readability:
★★★★
orgasm rating:
♀♀♀
orgasm rating:
♂
speed:
★★★
UK

http://www.aristasia.org

Aristasia – The Feminine Nation

Aristasia is a feminine empire, free of men and free of all that is sordid about the modern world. At first glance it may also appear to be free of reason, but delve deeper and you may find something worthwhile. The creation of Marianne Martindale, Aristasia exists as a concept in the same way as a Tolkienesque fantasy world exists, with provinces, cities, history and all. To try to understand it is necessary to visit the site, which combines an old-fashioned charm with misandrist lesbianism and corporal punishment. To put it another way, if you are a girl who likes the idea of being caned while dressed up in immaculate clothing of any period from the Victorian to the 1950s, then Aristasia could be the place for you. The site is large, verbose, and confusing to navigate, but worthwhile all the same.

SPECIAL FEATURES

Blonde and Brunette are the Aristasian sexes, replacing female and male, and much the same as femme and butch, only in a nicer way.

The Blue Camellia Club is the Aristasian message board.

Aristasia, Fact or Fantasy provides a full explanation of the Aristasian ethos.

The Provinces of Aristasia features the map and explanation of the fantasy empire. Each province corresponds to a period of real world history. Quirinelle, for instance, reflects the 1950s, and Vintesse the 1920s. Time stops at 1963, with the introduction of such horrors as tights in place of stockings.

Glossary of Aristasian Terms lists a complete terminology, much of it designed to enable Aristasians to look down on the real world. 'Bongo' means anything related to 'The Pit', which refers to modern times, the 'decades of darkness since the eclipse', said 'eclipse' referring in turn to the 'cultural and spiritual collapse of the early 1960s'. 'Silly Monkeys' are SMers; that is, those who do as the Aristasians do but not in the same context.

Sweethearts is the most practical area of the site: a girls only club in the Aristasian style, meeting at the Candy Bar on the first Sunday of every month. Lipstick, stockings, scent, and lace are de rigeur.

OTHER FEATURES

The site is large and contains internal links to various related areas, but has no outgoing links or other features relating to the real world.

The Aristasian empire, for corporal punishment of old-fashioned girls and more.

Section 07

the hard stuff

There can be no doubt that the commonest type of sex sites on the net are picture galleries aimed at heterosexual men. Of the thousands of choices available we have selected ten in the vain hope of providing a representative sample. Only two are paysites, the rest are free. While we felt we should cover a couple of the largest and best paysites, this is an area where you can get by very well without paying a penny.

Free picture sites come and go, but we have done our best to chose well established examples. The majority of sites take a positive or even worshipful attitude to the women they portray, and we have avoided those which take a racist or misogynist view. Net porn is designed to stimulate at a pretty basic level, so do not go in expecting artistic or sensitive portrayals of sexuality.

JARGON

Net porn has developed its own jargon, largely based on American slang. This is fairly consistent but can be confusing. Still, once you've realised that 'ass' has nothing to do with donkeys, you should get along well enough. The jargon is often crude and may be offensive, so if you are of a sensitive nature, beware. A few terms are worth a note.

***Thumbnail gallery*: A gallery of small pictures each of which is a link to a larger version of the same picture. This can be an excellent way to**

view dirty pictures, but occasionally just clicking on a small picture will take you somewhere unexpected, generally in the hope of luring you into a paysite. Again, how anyone can possibly expect such a cheap trick to succeed is beyond us.

Teen: A common obsession with sex sites. 'Teen' does not mean underage girls, but girls of 17 to 19, depending on the age of consent in the country where the site is hosted. The same applies to terms such as 'Schoolgirl' and 'Lolita'. Some sites do specialise in genuine teenage models, others simply use 'Teen' to draw in the punters.

Cheerleaders: One of the favourite themes for US sex sites, the great majority of cheerleader shots are simply of models stripping out of cheerleader uniforms. Perhaps one picture in a hundred is a genuine candid cheerleader shot.

Black/Blonde/Redhead: Picture galleries are often divided according to the physical characteristics of the models, often their racial origin.

Voyeur: A common theme, showing sneaky shots or supposedly sneaky shots of girls on the beach, by looking through windows, with hidden cameras or up women's skirts. Some of these are genuine, more are posed. Such activity can be offensive or even illegal.

Exhibitionist: Public flashing must have increased a hundred-fold since it became possible to post pictures on the net. This is one of the few areas where the genuine content exceeds the fake, and anyone who likes the idea of girls, or men, showing off their assets in a public place will find the net a positive goldmine.

Amateur: A misleading term, mostly. You might hope that 'amateur' would mean someone who likes to show off just for the fun of it. Usually it means someone who is not actually a fully paid-up member of the sex industry but still charges for the pleasure of seeing them naked. Most 'amateur' sites are women's homepages which require membership for access. These often have a personal feel to them which some enjoy. Genuine amateurs are more often labelled as exhibitionists.

Lesbian: Very seldom means pictures of women whose sexual preference is for other women. Far more often it means posed shots of professional female models having sex together for the gratification of a largely male audience.

Asian: A common category almost always meaning Japanese. Next to the US, Japan has the strongest presence among net sex sites and also a distinctive style. Pet obsessions include bondage, school uniforms, and watersports. Many UK surfers who get on quite happily with US sites may find Japanese sites disturbing.

Celebrity: Might be expected to mean candid shots of film stars, pop stars, and the like, especially those who posed nude before their careers took off. To some extent this is true, and anyone wanting nude pictures of Geri Halliwell or Madonna will do fine. 'Celebrity' also includes porn stars, professional nude models, and other sex workers, very few of whom the average UK surfer will ever have heard of.

Fetish: May mean a lot or very little. Some sites include such mainstream pleasures as fellatio under fetish.

BDSM: Bondage, Domination, Sadism and Masochism, often all lumped together for convenience.

Facials: A common category that has nothing to with skin treatment and everything to do with men coming over women's faces.

Anal: Means what it says, for once.

overall rating:
★★★★★
classification:
free gallery
updated:
frequently
navigation:
★★★★★
content:
★★★★
readability:
★★★
orgasm rating:
♀♀♀
orgasm rating:
♂♂♂♂
speed:
★★★★
US

http://bootyranch.com

The Bootyranch

A big, slick site with hundreds of free pictures of naked girls. The galleries are in categories and show a bit more flair than usual, with a few unusual headings. There is a laddish feel to it, and we found describing big girls as 'heifers' rather off-putting, but at least they're there, as are transvestites. The content is softcore and well presented, but we found some of the thumbnails too small, and the format is inconsistent. Netscape with Javascript enabled is recommended, and the navigation is flawless. Unlike so many free sites, there are few distracting banners, although it is a courtesy to at least click on the sponsor's adverts.

SPECIAL FEATURES

Fifteen categories are offered, according to sexual taste, but with titles that may confuse. The straightforward categories are: Bikini, Butts (that's girls' bottoms to us Brits, not large water containers), Lingerie, Black Girls, Booty (general nude body shots), Beach Bunnies, and Asian. More specialised galleries cover Cowgirls (sometimes just girls with their jeans pulled down), Bi-TV, French Postcards (stylised erotica from the 1920s, Heffers (sic) (big girls, right up to very big girls), and a specialist gallery of sixties-style nudes. There is also an art gallery presenting the original artwork of Helmut Preiss, which may be purchased direct or commissioned. These are soft, sensuous pictures of women, somewhat stylised, and done in a variety of media. A wide variety of collectors' magazines is also offered.

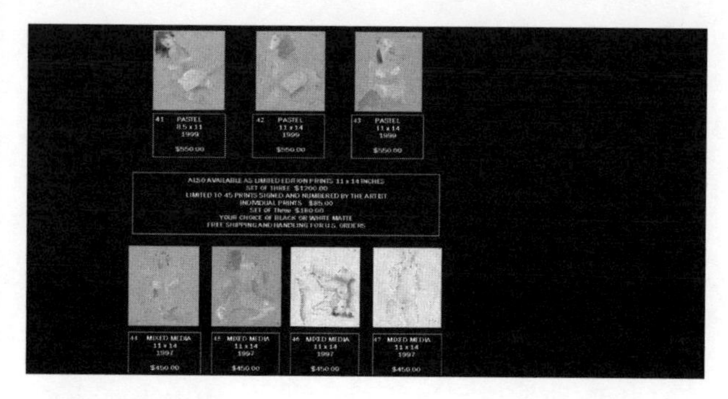

OTHER FEATURES

Links and a search facility are offered. The site can be emailed.

A good, free softcore site with a little extra style.

overall rating:
★★★★★
classification:
commercial sex
updated:
daily
navigation:
★★★★★
content:
★★★★★
readability:
★★★★★
orgasm rating:
♀♀
orgasm rating:
♂♂♂♂♂
speed:
★★★★★
DENMARK £

http://www.colorclimax.com

Color Climax

A large, professional site from the Color Climax Corporation. Very well presented, with everything from sexy poses to full hardcore. Twenty-five dollars buys a month's membership, $65 three months' membership, paid through a secure credit card link. A preview is offered, and a choice of languages from English, French, German, Spanish and Japanese. Within the site, six studios are offered according to subject. The focus is as much on individuals as on what they're doing, which we liked, and while the models are clearly professional, there is more realism than with many sites. Navigation is easy, the content good, and broad, with thumbnails bringing up big, high resolution pictures. What you really pay for is their professionalism.

SPECIAL FEATURES

The site presents eight studios, based on their publications and with a good deal of overlap between them. These are: Color Climax, Blue Climax, School Girls, Anal Sex, Lesbian Love, Sex Bizarre, Transexual Climax, and Climax Gold. Within each, photo-sets and movies may be accessed by subject or by the names of models. Each model is presented with a biography and links to her photosets, which vary from simple poses to hardcore, right up to watersports (that's peeing on each other, not messing about in boats). We took a look at Tiny Tove, a pretty, petite girl from the School Girls studio who used to be a

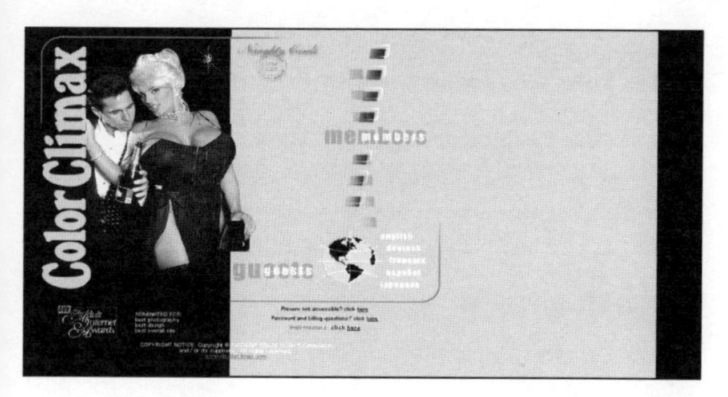

Color Climax favourite. She was featured in three galleries which we thought pretty hot stuff, both rude and realistic, along with five movies around seven minutes long each.

OTHER FEATURES

Erotic Art and Naughty Cards are also featured.

A high quality professional site, with good porn and lots of it for your money.

overall rating:
★★★★
classification:
free specialist gallery
updated:
frequently
navigation:
★★★★
content:
★★★★
readability:
★★★
orgasm rating:
♀♀♀♀
orgasm rating:
♂♂♂♂
speed:
★★★
US

http://www.eezzii.com

Babble-On

Babble-On is not the largest site for fans of voyeurism and exhibitionism, but it is free and genuine. The morality may be questionable, but it's hard to deny the thrill of taking a sneaky peek. Babble-On provides plenty of these, and if the style is a touch crude, it is also upbeat and enthusiastic. The site design is not all it might be, while there are too many advertising banners, but all in all we thoroughly enjoyed out visit.

SPECIAL FEATURES

Hidden Camera Pics are four series of pictures taken from a miniature camera hidden in a drum kit. These show the host making love to three single girls as well as in a threesome, and appear to be genuine. Clearer pictures are available on any hardcore site, but not with that frisson of the illicit. We weren't sure if Alan, the host, deserved patting on the back or punching, but neither of us could deny getting a kick out of the pictures.

Voyeur Pics are four galleries, consisting of 20 pictures each, showing sneaky shots of girls. Some are just inadvertent flashes of knickers, while others are stronger. Some looked posed, which for us spoilt the effect, but others are clearly genuine, and once again we found ourselves rather guiltily enjoying the show. One we particularly enjoyed was of a woman with her breasts showing through a soaked sports top and a cross expression directed towards the camera.

Exhibitionist Galleries No guilt here, with nine women and three men deliberately showing off for the camera. All appear to be genuine amateurs, which we liked. Inevitably, the quality of photos is variable, and the content varies from dull to deliciously titillating. The females seemed more imaginative and more inclined to tease, the males simply to make a demonstration of their virility.

Babble-On's Bedtime Stories is a collection of five fairly straightforward erotic short stories, complete with illustrations.

OTHER FEATURES

Babble-On also invites contributions and offers space to voyeurs and exhibitionists. The site also hosts a bulletin board and a chatroom. A few general erotic links are listed.

A good free site for lovers of voyeurism and exhibitionism. Genuine and enthusiastic.

overall rating:
★★★★
classification:
free gallery
updated:
frequently
navigation:
★★★★★
content:
★★★★
readability:
★★★★
orgasm rating:
♀♀
orgasm rating:
♂♂♂♂
speed:
★★★★
US

http://www.boobland.com

Boobland

Boobland is what free picture sites ought to be: fast, friendly, and easy to use, with hundreds of pictures, the minimum of banners, and no misleading links. Here the porn-surfer can look at an impressive selection of girls and couples in large, high-resolution pictures. The bulk of the content is soft, but uninhibited, with pretty models posing naked or near-naked. A quarter or so of the pictures are relatively hardcore, with couples and threesomes shown enjoying all the usual kinds of sex. From the title you might expect the content to be devoted to large-breasted girls, but it's actually pretty general. It's slick, professional, straightforward, and largely for the boys. You enter the site by scrolling down the homepage to 'Enter Boobland'.

SPECIAL FEATURES

The site is divided into four major picture categories, principally according to skin colour, and each category is split into New Galleries and Last Rotation, with new pictures being added at reasonable intervals. The categories are white, black, and latino, which speak for themselves. Twenty selected pictures are also shown and rotated daily. The Lesbian and Hardcore section shows straightforward sex acts, with an emphasis on girls playing with other girls. These are professional, and fans of amateurs may find it all a bit artificial.

OTHER FEATURES

Links and recommendations for other free sites are also included, along with adverts, and it is possible to email the site with your comments.

Good, straightforward smut, free and well presented. One for the lads.

overall rating:
★★★★
classification:
free gallery
updated:
frequently
navigation:
★★★★
content:
★★★★★
readability:
★★★★
orgasm rating:
♀♀♀
orgasm rating:
♂♂♂♂♂
speed:
★★★★
US

http://www.cum123.com

CUM 123

The moment of male orgasm is a favourite topic of hardcore sites, with the emphasis on what is charmingly known as the 'facial'. For the vast majority of men and a good proportion of women there is something wonderful about the moment a man comes. For men this may be the display of virility, for women the implications of impregnation, but without delving too far into the complexities of human sexual behaviour, we felt we needed to include such a site. Dedicated sites and sections of sites abound, but we chose CUM 123 because is it simple, friendly, and free. With 14 galleries and over 400 pictures there is plenty to see, with every imaginable variation on the theme included. The navigation is fast enough, and the picture quality is generally good. There are quite a few commercial banners, but they do not swamp the site.

SPECIAL FEATURES

This is a straightforward site which delivers what it promises, no more, no less. Fourteen galleries are listed, but in a line, so that only nine show at any one time. Thirty thumbnails are included in each gallery, and each one is large and sharp enough to give a clear idea of what you will get if you click for the big picture. Many of the pictures are sequences, and the majority are oral and focused on the woman. We liked the fact that almost all the girls are happy, smiling and obviously playing to the camera, although some may find this gives a false feeling to the pictures.

OTHER FEATURES

A guestbook is offered, as well as a few somewhat random links.

Free hardcore cum shots, simple, easy to use and satisfyingly dirty.

overall rating:
★★★★
classification:
free gallery
updated:
daily
navigation:
★★★★
content:
★★★★
readability:
★★★
orgasm rating:
♀♀♀
orgasm rating:
♂♂♂♂
speed:
★★★★
US

http://www.lesbians4free.com

Lesbians 4 Free

Lesbians 4 Free is a big free gallery site specialising in pictures of girls posing together and having sex together. On the net 'lesbian' is used to mean pretty girls posing or playing together for mainly male enjoyment far more often than in the sense of women who have an active sexual preference for other women. Certainly, Lesbians 4 Free is not what we'd think of as a genuine lesbian site, but it does contain a lot of pictures of girls having sex. Such sites are common on the net, but we chose this one because it is large and well presented, with the minimum of advertising and paysite links. We found the style a little crude and laddish, but far less so than many sites.

SPECIAL FEATURES

Galleries are the main feature of the site. Many are reached by a thumbnail on the main page, others by a text link. In both cases you reach a thumbnail gallery, and although we didn't count, many hundreds of pictures must be included on the site. Most galleries feature a photoset of two or more girls having sex, and a minority have individual shots. The photos are clear, high quality, and full of smiling models doing rude things to each other. Some content is hardcore although not extreme. Several galleries have weekly updates of the same models in different scenarios. We took a look at Laura and Amy's sex-toy photo set to find two pretty young blonde girls playing with a vibrator. Nothing is hidden, but we would have liked a bit more passion.

In general we were quite impressed by the content, although it is obviously posed, so this is not a site for lovers of amateurs.

Links are extensive, mostly with a brief description of content and mainly to sites that feature girls together, exclusively or in part. The majority of these are free, and there are so many and the updates so frequent that the site makes a good starting point for any surfers wanting this speciality.

OTHER FEATURES

A few more general links are offered, and the site can be emailed.

A good free gallery site for girls playing with girls.

overall rating:
★★★★
classification:
free gallery
updated:
frequently
navigation:
★★★★
content:
★★★★
readability:
★★★
orgasm rating:
♀
orgasm rating:
♂♂♂
speed:
★★★★
US

http://www.nudecelebritypics.com

Nude Celebrity Pics

Kylie Minogue sunbathing topless? Geri Halliwell in a fishnet body stocking? Nude Celebrity Pics has it all; a site dedicated to what has become a major obsession on the net. They claim to be the largest nude celebrity site on the net. Certainly they are one of the few free ones among an enormous number of paysites. Even here, you have to wade through a page of banners and links to nude celebrity paysites before you get to a fast and well-designed jump station. Don't click on anything until you reach the bottom of the page. Inside there are softcore pictures, of women only, and the thrill comes mainly from their status, but perhaps also because not all of them are happy about their pictures being on world-wide distribution. Having said that, we only recognised about one name in 10, but maybe they're famous in the US.

SPECIAL FEATURES

Although this is a basic gallery site, it is so large that the main section is broken down alphabetically for ease of use. The Celebrities category covered 1,219 women and 2,393 pictures when we visited. Other categories are Pornstars, Singers, SportBabes, SI Models, Young Actresses, Models, Girls of Melrose Place, Girls of 90210, Classic Actresses, Baywatch, and B Movie Actresses. Quite a few women appear in more than one category, but generally with different pictures. Going into the Celebrity area, we got to the Celebz A-Z, finding each girl with up to three pictures. There are no thumbnails, but clicking on the name you want leads to the photos, which vary from large and clear to small and grainy. We failed to recognise the majority of names but tried Geri Halliwell, finding a choice of her pre-Spice Girls nude shots. She was also listed in the Singers category, with different pictures from the same era. Kylie Minogue yielded one nicely posed but coy nude and two pictures of her topless on a beach and looking pretty fed up, presumably because she knew the paparazzi had got her.

OTHER FEATURES

Extensive links are provided, but exclusively to those paysites that sponsor this site and keep it free.

A large gallery site dedicated to female celebrities.

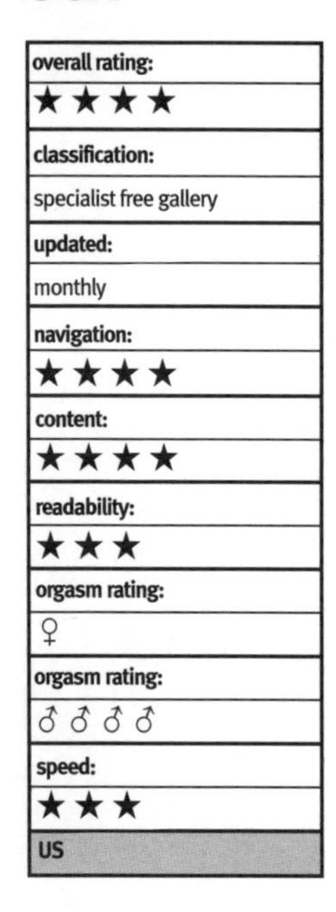

overall rating:
★★★★
classification:
specialist free gallery
updated:
monthly
navigation:
★★★★
content:
★★★★
readability:
★★★
orgasm rating:
♀
orgasm rating:
♂♂♂♂
speed:
★★★
US

http://www.pantygirl.com

Panty Girl

Girls in panties are perhaps the most popular softcore speciality on the web, and hundreds of sites exist. We chose Panty Girl because it's free, personal, and full of enthusiasm. It also provides a great starting point for any porn-surfer after pictures of girls in just their panties. The site is rather cluttered with advertising banners, and we found that some links had been taken down to save space. We liked it anyway, but while bisexual women and lesbians may enjoy a visit, it is really one for the boys.

SPECIAL FEATURES

Newsletter welcomes you to the site and also covers updates.

Picture Gallery contains plenty of softcore pictures, featuring the Panty Girl in a huge range of poses and clothes. These were cute and sexy but soft. Each gallery is thumbnailed, leading to fair-sized, clear pictures. Nikki, from the Pantybabes paysite, is also featured, along with samples from other panty sites for variety. Six video clips from Pantybabes.com are also featured.

Bio This is the biography of Julie, the Panty Girl herself, a bubbly American blonde twentysomething. This gives the site a personal touch, and we learn not just her measurements and what sort of panties she likes to wear, but also her hobbies, ambitions, and love of cheesecake (but only a little at a time).

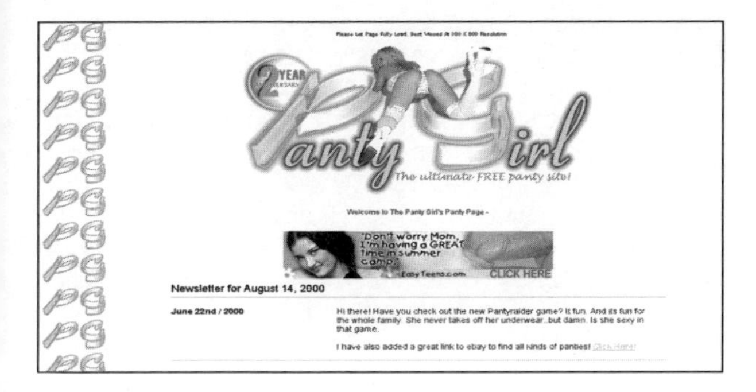

Questionnaire provides an opportunity to give detailed feedback and influence future updates to the site.

OTHER FEATURES

Extensive links are also provided, if not in very clear form.

A fine site if you like girls in just their panties.

overall rating:
★★★★
classification:
commercial sex
updated:
daily
navigation:
★★★
content:
★★★★
readability:
★★★★
orgasm rating:
♀♀
orgasm rating:
♂♂♂♂
speed:
★★★★
US £

http://www.penthouse.com

Penthouse.com

Slick, professional, and huge, there is no doubt that the Penthouse site is among the biggest and best on the net. Our considered opinion, reached after many, many hours of surfing, is that you should never need to pay for sex on the net. That said, if you really must, then this is the sort of site to go for. A free tour is offered, designed simply to tempt you to join. If you do, $19.95 per month (easily paid for on a UK credit card) gets you complete access to this huge collection of photos, videos, stories, and much more. Other affiliated sites are also accessible. The site was a bit cluttered, and there was also too much jargon for easy navigation. There is a contrived feel to it all, but really, for straightforward porn, this is as good as it gets.

SPECIAL FEATURES

The Photo Gallery is the mainstay of the site, presenting a huge, exclusive collection of posed models split into 15 sub-categories according to content. These include pets, couples, various groups, hardcore, fetish, and even pee. All the photos are big, high-resolution, and professional, but not really for those who like their sex down to earth. A peep into the 37-gallery fetish section revealed a beautiful girl licking the shoe of a whip-wielding dominatrix... Very pretty, but hardly realistic. Do these people have any idea what a five-foot single thong lash can do?

Strongbox This is a hardcore photo series, showing penetration and all but the more extreme sex acts, again in situations that seemed somewhat contrived.

Videoplex features real-time videos, some over an hour long, which play in a small box on your screen. Sexy, naughty stuff, but with a lot less impact than on a full screen.

Hot Reading These are commissioned stories of a higher quality than most of the net's dirty-story content.

Penthouse Variations is a similar ezine running in parallel.

Fun and Games features sexy computer games such as answering trivia questions to see progressively naughtier pictures.

Smart Sex and Penis Page offer advice on sexual health and safety issues.

OTHER FEATURES

What's New, Interviews, an Agony Aunt, and client services are all offered, along with occasional features such as the Houston 500 Gangbang; one girl and an awful lot of men!

A top paysite for softcore and light hardcore.

overall rating:
★★★
classification:
free gallery
updated:
occasionally
navigation:
★★★
content:
★★★★
readability:
★★★
orgasm rating:
♀♀
orgasm rating:
♂♂♂♂
speed:
★★★★
US

http://www.ebonyisland.com

Ebony Island

Ebony Island specialises in pictures of black women. This is one of the more popular specialist topics for internet porn, and we chose this site for size and variety of content. The style is rather neutral, with no real sense of individuality, but if the site is mainly designed to lead into related paysites, then that doesn't stop you enjoying it for free. Navigation is reasonably fast, but there are too many banners and commercial adverts, including a page of adverts before you enter the main site. Some of these are designed to be deliberately misleading, although there were no annoying pop-up windows. To enjoy the site, surf with care.

SPECIAL FEATURES

This is a simple gallery site. When we visited there were 46 galleries containing well over 400 pictures in all. Each gallery is thumbnailed, although in some cases the thumbnails are so small that we couldn't work out what was happening in the picture. The content is very variable, with black models being the only thing all the pictures have in common. We felt this to be both the strength and the weakness of the site. On the one hand some pictures are very small or of poor quality. On the other hand, the variety is impressive, with girls of every shape and size, and many amateurs. Candid shots are included, and even fully-clothed photos of sexy black women in the street, along with softcore and hardcore poses. This variety gives the site content a down-to-earth feel which we enjoyed, although if you want only posed pictures of thin and immaculately made up professional models, then this site is not for you. There were also four guest galleries from the paysite Ebony Fantasy.

OTHER FEATURES

The site can be emailed. A free adult chat link is offered, which goes to a general chat server rather than an onsite facility.

Plenty of variety for those who like sexy black girls.

Section 08

cybersex

At first glance interactive net sex appears to offer a wonderful world of free and safe erotic entertainment. At second glance it is a minefield of technical problems and scams. It is, unfortunately, but with care and patience it is possible have a great deal of fun without going bankrupt.

The first rule to success is to be patient, with hardware, software, and above all with other people. Go in like a bull at a gate and you'll end up with a sore head. Take it slowly, read background information, and make sure you know what you are doing. Once you are in you can either pay and hope to get what you pay for, or do your best to get it for free.

There are plenty of variations on interactive net sex, from simply swapping emails and using systems like AOL instant messenger with existing friends, right up to large-scale commercial videoconferencing. We identified five main areas.

***Information exchange* is the basic form of interactive net sex, with adult orientated information being passed among groups of people who share similar interests. The main forum for this is in the newsgroups, which have evolved so that a group exists for just about every topic imaginable. These used to work well, but they have now become flooded with so much spam that if you sign up to one you will probably get 50 unwanted adverts to every relevant message. Using**

newsgroups is also a common way to pick up computer viruses.

Chat allows you to communicate with others in real time. Users operate in a chatroom, in which many people can discuss whatever they please. The technicalities of chat can look pretty terrifying, but in practice your browser is probably set up to cope with all but the most obscure systems and even these can generally be downloaded as and when necessary. The commonest system is now IRC (Internet Relay Chat), for which there are many thousand channels. Most chatrooms that are offered by sites use IRC, and any browser with Java enabled should connect you without difficulty.

Once in, you do need to understand a few basic commands to get the most out of chat. Commands vary between systems, but will be provided on the chat window in each case. When new it is a good idea to say so. People will then make allowances while you learn your way around.
Unlike adult keywords, chat-related keywords work on search engines and there are plenty of sites offering advice on chat. We chose to review www.whozit.com which covers just about everything you could ever want to know.

Video chat follows the same basic rules as chat, but you need a camera and a program that will allow you to send and receive video. Audio may also be included. www.4-video-sex.com is a useful general resource for all matters relating to video sex. The two main systems for video chat are CUseeMe and Netmeeting. If you have either of these programs but no camera, you can 'lurk', joining in a session without transmitting an image, although this may make you unpopular with other users.

CUseeMe is well established. Two programs are available: freeware originally developed by Cornell University, and a commercial version developed by White Pines. For information and free download of the Cornell version, visit cuseeme.net, or www.cuseeme.com for the White Pines versions starting at $69. We had considerable technical trouble with the Cornell version, which caused both Windows and Mac systems to crash with three separate operators. CUseeMe sites are referred to as Reflectors. Many adult CUseeMe reflectors are paysites.

Netmeeting is the Microsoft video system and comes as standard with most Microsoft software packages. We had no difficulty installing or using it. The only drawback is that the system is less well established and so there are fewer, less specialist channels. For information go to www.microsoft.com/windows/netmeeting, which also provides a list of public ILS (Internet Locator Server) sites. Netmeeting may be used through these or directly between individuals.

Webcams provide links from a video camera to your computer. In the case of adult webcams the camera is generally set up in a girl's bedroom. The majority of webcams are run by individuals and their style derives from the personality of the owner. Most require membership, especially those that guarantee nudity and promise sex shows. The most basic are free cams set up so that anybody interested can look in on the owner's life. Many of these have no nudity as a deliberate policy but may still provide a voyeuristic thrill.

With others nudity or even more is a possibility, but watchers may wait a very long time indeed for anything interesting to happen. Similar to these are live hidden cameras, which may be both morally indefensible and illegal, but exert an undeniable fascination. Genuine examples are rare.

To be sure of having any fun with a webcam it is really best to pay for one that guarantees adult content. Costs vary, but our review choice, Gina @ Britcam, works out at 22p per day, which is excellent value, especially in comparison to most net sex paysites. Most sites offer a preview area, and perhaps a free cam with a slow refresh rate or in a less exciting place, such as just outside the bedroom door so that viewers get just a hint of what is going on. At the least a picture of the owner will be provided, and webcam support sites such as The Peeping Moe allowing you to assess sites before visiting or joining up.

Grander and more expensive are full-scale commercial webcams. In some cases these cover whole houses with rent-free accommodation provided to any girls happy to be on camera. The idea is to provide a voyeuristic thrill by allowing users to watch people going about their daily lives, including intimate acts. However, girls may be paid for doing interesting things, such as taking a shower, so that you are effectively getting a paid show. Girls have been known to take 10 or more showers a day.

Generally, webcams do not provide real-time video but a series of pictures that refresh at regular intervals. The shorter these intervals, the better the experience, although both your computer system and all the connections involved must be capable of handling the amount of data being transmitted. Many webcams also provide a chat service so that you can communicate with the owner and other users. Some provide streaming, with audio in addition to video. Chatrooms will have monitors to prevent abusive behaviour.

Videoconferencing is a fully commercial development from webcams, where the user can watch or even direct a performance. This guarantees success, as you are paying a model or models directly, so is much the best option from the point of view of gratification. Not surprisingly it is also the most expensive option, and in our view seldom if ever represents good value. A typical charge would be £3 per minute, which works out to £180 per hour, for which you could quite happily hire the same performance for real and join in yourself.

With videoconferencing you are paying someone to perform for you, but that does not give you the right to be abusive. The site host can always cut you off. Be considerate, or at least nice. 'You're beautiful, please may I see your breasts' is more likely to get the right response than 'get your tits out', while 'strip, you bitch' will get you kicked off and probably banned. Remember, you are talking to a human being.

JARGON

While there is plenty of free or at least honest interactive net sex available, scams are common and users should approach with great care. The commonest is to offer free membership subject to handing over your credit card details to prove that you are an adult. You may then find that you get charged for 'premium services', which will include anything adult. The rates will be high, and you may not even realise you have been charged until you get the bill. Others may be more honest but still expensive.

Always remember, commerical paysites care a lot more about parting you from your money than providing entertainment. One large chat and video site even demanded $100 to allow us to review their site. We declined the offer.

'Live' may not always mean what it says. You may find you only receive a pre-recorded video and obviously no interaction with the model. 'Free', as always, is seldom what it seems.

JARGON

Lurkers People in video chatrooms with no camera who receive images but do not send them. This is generally felt to be impolite and untrustworthy. Many video chat facilities ban lurkers altogether, and lurking will always guarantee a poor reception. The commonest lurkers are men pretending to be women, often with some pretty pictures of a model ready to send to 'prove' their identity. In video chat, we found it very hard to trust anyone not prepared to send their image, especially as video hardware so cheap and easily available.

Abbreviations: These are commonly used in chat. They can vary, but a few of the commoner ones are worth a mention. BBL – be back later. BBN – bye bye now. BEG – big evil grin. CNP – continued in next post. CYA – see you. EMSG – email message. FYI – for your information. LOL – laughs out loud. WB – welcome back.

Spam: Unwanted advertising material, usually for get-rich-quick schemes or adult paysites. Going into anything that involves giving out your email address risks receiving spam, newsgroups especially. Viruses may come in with spam, and a good piece of advice is never to open anything that comes in on your mail as an attachment unless you know who it is from.

ETIQUETTE

Good behaviour on the net is much the same as in any other human social situation. The main difference is that more people are prepared to risk a virtual slap in the face than a real one. For this reason, abusive behaviour on the net is much more common than in real life.

For adult chat and video chat, tolerance, politeness, and patience are usually enough to ensure that you get on. Take care that you choose a chat facility in which adult chat is appropriate, or you are likely to be less than popular. Inevitably, there are people around who can't stand to see others having fun, so occasionally adult chatrooms will be invaded by people deliberately trying to spoil it for others. We have even seen websites detailing how to interfere with people trying to have cybersex! This is particularly true for minority interests. Gays and lesbians often suffer difficulties from homophobic people, while fetishistic sites may also be targeted by the intolerant.

While such people can be cut off and banned by monitors, they can still be a serious nuisance. False representation is also a problem. On the one hand, if you are in a chatroom you should not feel obliged to reveal the fact that you have a small but unsightly spot on your nose. On the other hand it is completely unreasonable to pretend to be female when you are in fact a man, although another school of thought holds that playing with sexual identities is what cybersex is all about. What is and is not acceptable will depend on the circumstances, but the best advice is to be who you are.

GOING REAL

If at any stage during an interactive net relationship you decide to meet somebody in the flesh, make sure you know exactly who you are dealing with before arranging a meeting. Many fine relationships have started on the net, but there are also many horror stories, in rare cases involving rape or even murder. Always ask for proof of identity, and do not be offended if you are asked the same in return. After all, if you are who you say you are then you have nothing to worry about. Don't listen to excuses.

First, ask to talk on the phone, which will give you a much better idea of the contact's personality than you get on the net. Anyone with access to a computer is going to have access to a phone, so if they refuse, be suspicious.

Some women's groups have devised questions to tell whether somebody is really female. These may weed out the least competent fakes but are not really reliable. Some men have managed to carry on full blown cybersex relationships with lesbian women for years without getting caught. Some may never have been caught.

Photographs mean very little unless they are customised. Ask your contact to pose standing by their street or town sign with an orange in each hand, or whatever. This sort of image is not going to be easily faked, and if they are too humourless to do it, then they're probably not worth meeting anyway. Don't let hope triumph over common sense.

Lastly, bring a friend along, even if you have to pay their expenses. It is not hard to cover up little personality defects, like being an axe-murderer, until you actually meet.

overall rating:
★★★★★
classification:
webcam homepage
updated:
constantly
navigation:
★★★★★
content:
★★★★★
readability:
★★★★
orgasm rating:
♀♀♀♀
orgasm rating:
♂♂♂♂♂
speed:
★★★★
UK

http://www.britcam.com

Gina @ Britcam

Rather than go for one of the big and glossy American webcams, we chose to review a private, British example. Gina @ Britcam was our choice, the webcam of a vivacious, pretty Yorkshire lass whose svelte body and friendly, mischievous character made her unmissable. The site contains both free and pay areas, with plenty of content other than the cam. Membership is £20 for three months or £10 per month, which is good value. The free cam refreshes every six minutes, the member's cam every 30 seconds. Content includes full nudity, so far featuring Gina on her own. Erotic striptease and masturbation are her specialities, with occasional mildly kinky content. The site is well designed, simple, efficient and advert-free. The style is personal, intimate, and ideal for this sort of site. True, it's really one for the boys, but we were both highly impressed.

SPECIAL FEATURES

Free Tour advertises the site and gives access to the free cam and pictures, including one of Gina kneeling in a bath full of milk and cereal.

Cam and Chat Gina uses a single cam and advertises the shows in her schedule, which generally number four to five shows of one to two hours each week. Having pre-arranged shows rather than random cams reduces the voyeuristic feel of the site, but does mean you get what you pay for. We visited Gina for her

Baby Oil show, logging onto her chatroom as well as the cam. Once we had downloaded a new chat server program everything went smoothly. Gina spent the first half-hour chatting and teasing the audience, which apparently numbered over 1,000. The chat was civilised, cool, and jokey at first, then heated and finally even a bit awestruck, but never unpleasant or insulting. Her show was subtle, intensely erotic, and slow in the nicest possible way. After an hour she was in nothing but a pair of crisp white panties and a lot of baby oil, then naked and masturbating happily on her bed until the end of the show. Chat continued long afterwards, with Gina in no hurry to close down.

Galleries Several galleries are presented, including webcam captures and Gina flashing in Scarborough. The video gallery requires RealPlayer, and includes a link to download this. Raindrops shows Gina laughingly stripping topless in the rain.

Stories is a new feature with one story from Gina and two from guests.

OTHER FEATURES

The site also includes personal information, links, support, a forum and contact details.

An excellent UK webcam and more.

overall rating:
★★★★★
classification:
lesbian service
updated:
frequently
navigation:
★★★★★
content:
★★★★★
readability:
★★★★★
orgasm rating:
not applicable
orgasm rating:
not applicable
speed:
★★★★
US

http://www.grrltalk.net

Muskie's Grrltalk

Grrltalk is a privately-run resource site for lesbian and lesbian-friendly chat areas. These are primarily IRC chat channels, and links are provided so that IRC software can be downloaded. Other chat facilities are listed and explained in detail. In fact, while Grrltalk is designed for use and the links provided are intended only for lesbians, the site also makes an excellent introduction to online chat. The design is simple, clear and easy to use, with a 'Clueless Newbies' guide for beginners. The chat facilities listed on Grrltalk are not necessarily designed for lesbian sex chat, and users should exercise discretion. We were highly impressed.

Note: In chat it is important to follow net etiquette. Lesbian chat in particular suffers from men pretending to be women and even hosting channels or rooms under false pretences. This is completely unreasonable behaviour and is, not surprisingly, resented. The offenders are nearly always straight men, who should think how they would feel if they arranged a date with someone who turned out to be another man.

SPECIAL FEATURES

Grrltalk is divided into two main areas:

Chat Listings covers an extensive range of links which are accessible by both type and subject. Advice is provided to steer newcomers through the difficulties of online chat and also on harrassment, in considerable technical detail. We looked at the Dalnet IRC listings, which alone covered 38 channels. Brief details of each channel are supplied, including those that are age restricted. For three of the channels, warnings are given that the channel manager is in fact a male posing as a female.

Community offers links to Grrltalk's own facilities, including bulletin boards, an infochat server, the Grrltalk chatroom at gay.com, and Grrltalk's Woman to Woman Personals. There are also links to personal homepages, the Dyke Test, and trivia games. Again, these are general facilities rather than specifically erotic ones. We looked at the homepage listings, which gave links to well over a hundred individual sites, including the hostess' own. Jenny also tried the Dyke Test and managed to score 84!

OTHER FEATURES

Grrltalk also includes a site map, a site search facility, and extensive related help and information.

A top resource for lesbian chat

overall rating:
★★★★★
classification:
service
updated:
frequently
navigation:
★★★
content:
★★★★★
readability:
★★★
orgasm rating:
not applicable
orgasm rating:
not applicable
speed:
★★★★
US

http://www.whozit.com

Whozit

Whozit is a general links site with a strong section for interactive links. From the mainpage, select Up Front and Personal for interactive sex site listings. The presentation is clear, with few adverts, although the sheer volume of information slows it down, and many of the text links are doubled up. In style it is enthusiastic, with a straightforward design and a simple jumpstation at the bottom of each page. While largely one for the boys, we felt it was in general a useful resource for interactive net sex.

SPECIAL FEATURES

Within the Up Front and Personal section, listings are split into Web/Chat and Personals:

Web/Chat covers 14 sub-categories and gives Whozit's top recommendations. Within the individual listings, each site is given with a text link and a brief commentary, with whatever interactive features it offers in italics. Inevitably, most of these are paysites, but webcams, chatrooms, IRC, phone sex, and shows are all there. The General Directory lists several hundred links, split into pages, each with a manageable number on them, listed alphabetically. With a little effort, everyone should be able to find what they are looking for, with sub-categories including gay and fetish sites.

Personals is split into no less than twenty sub-categories, although these do overlap. Some of the sites listed are international, but there is a strong US bias, and the feature is of limited use to UK surfers.

OTHER FEATURES

Whozit also provides a full range of features typical of a general links site.

A good general links site with an emphasis on interactive sites.

overall rating:
★★★★
classification:
video chat
updated:
constantly
navigation:
★★★★
content:
★★★★
readability:
★★★
orgasm rating:
♀♀♀♀
orgasm rating:
♂♂♂
speed:
★★★★
US

http://www.geocities.com/SouthBeach/Docks/2086/a-escape

An Escape

We chose An Escape as an example of a CUseeMe both for its friendly, welcoming atmosphere, and because it provides a useful introduction to CUseeMe etiquette. The site is simple and nicely designed, with a friendly, open style. The reflector IP, 24.13.241.140, is provided near the top of the mainpage.

SPECIAL FEATURES

Etiquette sets out a basic code of behaviour which not only applies to CUseeMe, but to all interactive adult net entertainment. This is given on the mainpage and should give anyone a clear idea of how to behave and not to behave during a live video chat session. Lurkers are not welcome, which is the case for the great majority of CUseeMe reflectors, especially free ones. Site monitors are present during sessions to moderate and either throw out or ban anybody abusing the system. At first glance this may seem off-putting, but An Escape is designed for adult interaction, though in a safe, non-abusive atmosphere. Downloading difficulties precluded full assessment of the site.

OTHER FEATURES

An Escape provides links to the owners' and moderators' homepages, although not all of these were up when we visited.

A free, friendly adult CUseeMe reflector site.

http://members.home.net/reflist

CUseeMe Reflectors and Links

This is a links site specifically for adult CUseeMe Reflectors and related subjects. Although not an erotic site as such, it makes a good starting point for anybody interested in CUseeMe. The site has a somewhat amateur feel, but is efficient and generally fast, with a simple jumpstation at the top of the mainpage. We did feel it might have been bigger and a bit more exciting, but it does its job.

Note: Always follow good etiquette when on CUseeMe. There is no guarantee of nudity on CUseeMe, and you should not expect other users to necessarily behave the way you want them to.

overall rating:
★★★★
classification:
specialist service
updated:
occasionally
navigation:
★★★★★
content:
★★★★
readability:
★★★★
orgasm rating:
not applicable
orgasm rating:
not applicable
speed:
★★★★
US

SPECIAL FEATURES

The site divides links into five categories, three of which list reflectors. The links are set out in a clear, tabular form. Each reflector is listed with its name, channel address, and conference ID, along with any relevant information, emails and website addresses. Typically, a reflector will have a host and one or more monitors, who are responsible for maintaining etiquette. New reflectors are marked, as well as corrections to information.

Public Adult Refs is the largest section, covering over 100 active reflectors when we visited. Several inactive reflectors are also listed. These vary in size, popularity and style, and we recommend browsing.

Couples Refs is a much smaller list, with 17 reflectors catering specifically for couples.

Single Sex Refs are reflectors specifically for gay men and lesbians. Thirty-seven were listed, mainly for gay men, and many were local to areas within the US.

Pay Sites gives links to websites hosting reflectors for which membership is required. Many of these are general interactive sites and may include reflectors where sexual content is guaranteed. Twenty-four sites were listed.

Links covers general CUseeMe sites, including those that provide detailed information on the topic, and both Cornell University and White Pines Software, from which free and commercial versions of CUseeMe may be downloaded respectively.

OTHER FEATURES

The site also provides some advice on CUseeMe. Information on reflector sites may be sent in.

A good basic resource site for CUseeMe.

http://ils.demon.co.uk

Demon ILS Server

overall rating:
★★★★
classification:
video service
updated:
constantly
navigation:
★★★★★
content:
★★★★
readability:
★★★★
orgasm rating:
♀♀♀♀♀
orgasm rating:
♂♂♂
speed:
★★★★
UK

Having chosen Netmeeting as our preferred video system, we chose the UK ILS (Internet Locator Server) from Demon. Microsoft Netmeeting must be correctly set up on your computer for this to work, and can be downloaded via a link, although most up-to-date Windows systems will include it as a standard feature. Demon ILS is fast, simple, and foolproof. What matters is what happens once you're connected.

SPECIAL FEATURES

From the mainpage the site gives two simple options:

Find Everyone Online is the basic feature, listing all users currently online along with details. This gives name, location (which may be blank), email address, and the Netmeeting box if you want to connect. The internal Netmeeting list is more detailed, and includes whether each user has audio and/or video. We visited at midnight to find well over 100 people available, most of whom were after adult interaction. Of these the great majority were single males, with a few couples and single females. A small proportion were gay men, while about half the single women wanted another woman. Jenny took over the keyboard and entered her details as a single female, which provoked an immediate torrent of calls. Each call rings, and you may answer or not, with your picture going out only if you chose to accept the call. Click on 'Ignore' if you're not interested.

Alternatively, you can dial out, either by double clicking on the user's name or the dialling symbol. Jenny altered her details to couples and single females only, although this didn't make much difference to the number of single males trying to get through. She quickly learnt that many 'girls' without cams are in fact men, and that with 'couples' the female partner is often in bed early/away/just putting the cat out. After a frustrating half-hour, Jenny managed to connect to Lucy from Vienna, a petite blonde girl who was already stark naked. Lucy had no audio, but communicated via the Netmeeting text box. She wanted to see Jenny's breasts and it would have been unfair not to comply. Jenny spent the next hour trying to have virtual sex with Lucy, but slow connection speeds, camera and language problems made this difficult. Still, it was great fun, and doubtless practice makes perfect.

Specific Search allows you to type in the first part of an email address to see if a particular person is online.

OTHER FEATURES

Demon ILS also provide support and links to Internet Explorer and Microsoft Netmeeting.

A busy UK interactive video site.

http://ils.gaydar.co.uk

Gaydar Netmeeting

Gaydar Netmeeting is the ILS site for gaydar.co.uk. The site is absolutely straightforward, allowing quick access to gay video chat, the bulk of which is sexually explicit. Netmeeting is required. Clicking on Find Everyone Online lists those online, along with their details. To connect, double click on a name for a quick connection. Calls may or may not be accepted, and when you receive a call you can choose to accept it or ignore it.

overall rating:
★★★★
classification:
video service
updated:
constantly
navigation:
★★★★★
content:
★★★★
readability:
★★★★
orgasm rating:
♀
orgasm rating:
♂♂♂♂
speed:
★★★★
UK

SPECIAL FEATURES

Visitors to Gaydar can access either a complete list of those currently online or search by email address. We visited late at night to find over 50 men online. Nearly all of these were from the UK, with a few from the US, and even one man from Bogotá. The style was generally more overtly sexual and open than would be expected in a heterosexual video chat area. There was also a high proportion of users with cams, and all the users appeared to be entirely what they claimed. Most of the men were there specifically for video sex, with a few just wanting chat and some aiming to set up meetings in their home area. Not wanting to appear under false pretences, Matt went in as a researcher. Not surprisingly this did not produce a flood of eager calls, but those we did speak to were friendly and helpful. In general the site was active, and it makes a good resource for gay men interested in video chat.

OTHER FEATURES

All other features are on the main Gaydar site (see p.99 for full review).

An active UK gay video chat site.

http://naughtychat.com

Naughty Chat

overall rating:
★★★★
classification:
chat
updated:
constantly
navigation:
★★★★★
content:
★★★
readability:
★★★★
orgasm rating:
♀♀♀
orgasm rating:
♂♂♂
speed:
★★★★
US

Naughty Chat is a specialist adult chat service with over 200,000 registered users. The site is free and may be used by anyone who has created an account, a link for which is provided on the mainpage. The design is very clear, idiot-proof even, with help throughout so that anybody should be able to be chatting happily within a few minutes, no matter how computer-illiterate. Once inside, you will find that the majority of users and regulars know each other. Newcomers will find it a bit like joining a new social group, with the important difference that if you don't get on well you can rejoin under a different identity! In terms of actual sexual content we weren't too impressed. Most of the chat is casual, although it can get very steamy indeed. The majority of users are American, so their evening is the middle of the night for the UK, which can be awkward. Nevertheless, as an adult chat site, this is as good as any.

SPECIAL FEATURES

Naughty Chat has a good many rooms, including private rooms that can be created individually. Eight rooms can be accessed direct from the mainpage. These include:

The Naughty Chat Lobby This is the main room and generally the busiest. When we visited there was plenty going on. In many ways it was like being at a real sex party, with an erotic buzz but not necessarily constant action. There are also similar social conventions and a tendency for the men to try and get the girls off to private rooms at the first opportunity.

Other Rooms includes specialist areas for gays, lesbians, and SMers, at least in theory. These are less busy, and users may find themselves alone or with people disinclined to speak. However, most of the best chat occurs in specialist rooms.

Transcripts gives a long list of past chat events, mainly with guest web hostesses from sex sites and professional models. These can get pretty heated, like the chat with Stormy from www.foxy14u.com which we looked at.

OTHER FEATURES

Naughty Chat also provides news, help features and an extensive mailing service. The Edit Profile feature allows users to give a customised description of themselves.

A free, high-quality adult chat facility.

http://www.peepingmoe.com

The Peeping Moe

The Peeping Moe is primarily a webcam listing and resource site. This is a free site, although the majority of cams listed are not free. The site is large, with extensive listings for all kinds of webcams. The basic design is excellent, and would be both efficient and clear if it weren't spoilt by advertising banners. Many of the banners are misleading and designed to appear to be integral parts of the site when they actually lead to paysites, so surf with care. Once you have got the hang of it, the site is great, with a framed jumpstation for access to the webcams. We had fun, but beware, it is possible to spend a lot of time here with very little to show for it, and it can be expensive.

overall rating:
★★★★
classification:
webcam directory
updated:
frequently
navigation:
★★★
content:
★★★★★
readability:
★★
orgasm rating:
♀♀♀
orgasm rating:
♂♂♂
speed:
★★★
US

SPECIAL FEATURES

Webcams makes up the bulk of the site, with cams listed as girls, guys, couples, and variety. Links are provided to the big webcams such as dormgirls, but the majority are owned by individuals. There are a great many of these, and they are listed alphabetically for each section. Every cam has an individual link page, with a picture of the owner, a mini-bio, and an assessment covering access, status, refresh rate, time zone, and amount of nudity. Many cams allow feedback to the owner. Not surprisingly, most of those cams showing nudity require membership, the cost of which varies.

Features covers site facilities, What's New, Galleries, and Shopping.

It also features Who's On Cam, which is invaluable to discover which webcams are actually online at any given time, although the information may sometimes be out of date.

Forums features discussions in general and of specific cams, some of which require ID check. These are valuable in that you can learn a lot about individual cams, particularly membership ones, before you visit or pay. Comments varied, including those who felt cheated, those disillusioned by the commercial nature of what they thought were personal cams, and those who had nothing but praise for their favourite cam owners. The StormDrain Forum is for those driven to exasperation by the whole business, a reaction we could well understand.

South Beach Archives is a photo archive of candid beach shots, mostly of girls sunbathing topless. Fun if you like voyeurism, but they're all much the same.

OTHER FEATURES

The Peeping Moe also offers general links, news, Moe products for sale, and an FAQ section and information for webmasters.

A great webcam listing and resource site.

http://www.plushhorse.com

Plush Horse

overall rating:
★★★★
classification:
videoconferencing
updated:
frequently
navigation:
★★★★
content:
★★★★
readability:
★★★★★
orgasm rating:
♀♀
orgasm rating:
♂♂♂♂♂
speed:
★★★★
US £

Plush Horse is a good example of an adult videoconferencing site. Not only does it appear attractive, but there is plenty of information for anyone new to the subject and to some extent the site can be used as a general videoconferencing resource. Plush Horse has been running since 1996, although the name has changed. Credit card details must be submitted to register, with the option of using a secure server. The site is clearly presented and professional, with less of the slick sales content than many such sites, and fast, readable, and easy to navigate.

Note: Videoconferencing can be very expensive.

SPECIAL FEATURES

The Models gives profiles of the models available for adult videoconferencing. Five were available when we visited, all attractive young women in erotic poses, but not naked. A user may call any model who is online and available, and she will perform to their instructions. Theoretically, there are no limits to this, and two girls may even be booked at the same time. Naturally, the girls set their own limits as to how far they will go. The site host admitted that the 'burn-out' rate of girls was high.

The Price is given clearly, which is not always the case with these sites. The basic price is $2.95 a minute, which allows video with teletyping of a single girl. Video with telephone is more expensive, and two girls double the price. All charges are discreetly billed as 'Jcom', and they accept MasterCard, Amex, and Visa. For telephone links international charges from the UK must be added to this, at anything from 6p a minute to 24p a minute (BT peak rate).

Register allows you to sign up for Plush Horse through a secure server if you want to. Full address, email, and credit card details are required. Registration may also be completed by phoning direct. Once registered, you will receive a list of numbers by email and may then use the services, for which your credit card will be debited.

Download lists the software necessary to use the service. Many new systems will already have this, otherwise links are provided to download a choice of four programs. For all of these Pentium 133 is a minimum requirement. Netmeeting is the preferred system.

Who's Online shows which models are currently available. Generally Plush Horse is open from 2pm to 2am Pacific Coastal time.

OTHER FEATURES

Plush Horse can be contacted direct, and provides technical help, a What's New feature, and links.

A high-quality US videoconferencing site

http://www.deja.com

deja.com

overall rating:
★★★
classification:
news groups
updated:
constantly
navigation:
★★
content:
★★
readability:
★★★
orgasm rating:
not applicable
orgasm rating:
not applicable
speed:
★★★
US

Deja.com is a general news site, but can be used as a resource for sex-related newsgroups. To do this, you need to click on Discussions on the mainpage to access Usenet and other forums. As the deja.com blurb says, this allows you to debate issues with millions of other people, including sex, but in reality the sheer volume of data available makes this no small task. The search facility will help with this, but do not expect an easy ride. The site design is fine, and the speed reasonable, but the difficulties inherent in newsgroups spoil deja.com as an interactive erotic site.

SPECIAL FEATURES

Newsgroup Listings Within deja.com, the majority of sex-related newsgroups are listed under the alt. category. Some of these link directly to the day's postings, while others link to further sub-categories. Underlined text in blue denotes links. Using the quick search bar we went to alt.sex, which listed 159 sub-categories. From there we went to alt.sex.fetish, which listed a further 48 sub-categories. Several of these listed further sub-categories, but we tried alt.sex.fetish.hair, hoping that it would prove to be an obscure enough topic to have avoided being swamped by spam. We were wrong. Of the 315 messages posted, nearly every one was an advert or a link to a paysite, and hardly any of these had anything to do with hair. Even those that did were mainly adverts for professional services. We found only one discussion on hair, and that turned out to be simply someone after a specific set of photos of a redhead. Again and again this proved to be the case, and we quickly became frustrated. It is theoretically possible to use deja.com to communicate with like minded people on newsgroups, but it is certainly not easy, and we would recommend alternative methods. The risk of downloading viruses from message attachments is also high.

OTHER FEATURES

Deja.com also offers advanced search facilities and free membership for those wishing to post membership and join discussion groups.

A news site including listings of sex-related newsgroups. Theoretically a great resource, but ruined by spam.

up close & personal

Net sex is fine, but when you find yourself going deathly pale and the use of your legs starts to fade you might actually want to meet other people. Plenty of internet sites specialise in contact services, while many British clubs designed for meeting people with similar interests have websites. In making our selection we have tried to be broad, including something for everybody.

This was hardest for the mainstream, where there is little sense of sexual community and by and large people have to get on as best they may. Heterosexual adults seeking partners are best off with contact sites, and it could be argued that the world at large is their meeting venue. Swingers do better from the net, with plenty of clubs and contact services to chose from.

Gay men and lesbians both have well established communities in Britain, and this is reflected on the net. Fetishists also do well, as the UK has the world's busiest and best fetish and BDSM community. There are even plenty of resources for those who are gay or bisexual and into SM as well.
The same advice applied on meetings as given in the previous chapter. Within the UK's swinging, gay, lesbian and SM communities many

people know each other and it is often possible to get an idea of what somebody is like before meeting them alone. For both the swinging and heterosexual SM scenes, there is always a surplus of single men. Women, particularly single women, are always in high demand and can sometimes find the experience overwhelming. For single men to succeed we have four pieces of advice:

- Find a partner outside the scene and explore it together.
- Be somebody, do something, anything, just don't be one more face in the crowd.
- Work on your social skills before worrying about your sexual skills
- Oh, and when you're out there for goodness sake practise safe sex.

http://www.sexyduo.gothere.uk.com

Dean and Matty's Swinging Contacts

We chose Dean and Matty as a good example of a personal contact site. Essentially this is a homepage expanded to form a contact site for the sake of others who enjoy the same lifestyle as the host and hostess. The site is entirely free, and we liked their style, which is open, honest and friendly. Adequately fast, easy to navigate and pretty well free of irritating banners, this site is a pleasure to use.

overall rating:
★★★★★
classification:
contacts
updated:
constantly
navigation:
★★★★★
content:
★★★★★
readability:
★★★★★
orgasm rating:
not applicable
orgasm rating:
not applicable
speed:
★★★★
UK

SPECIAL FEATURES

Bio Page has brief descriptions of the couple, their likes and dislikes, and an offer to get in touch if you think you would fit in and want to play.

Swingers Ads is the heart of the site, with ads listed in eight categories. Females and couples are invited to seek other females, males, couples and groups. Single males are not invited to participate, which reflects the reality of the swinging scene. We looked at females seeking couples and found six listed, then at females seeking females, with 12 listed. Every one had included a photo, and after looking at Louise from Wales, we decided that what the contacts lack in quantity they probably make up for in quality.

Swingers Galleries features extensive galleries of swingers using the site, mostly naked or half-naked. Designed to link in with the ads.

Post Your own Ad provides details for putting up your own ad.

Adult Gifts offers a selection of animated adult gifts for your amusement.

OTHER FEATURES

The site also offer links, both to swinging sites and others they enjoy, a chatroom, a swingers' forum, and a list of swingers on ICQ. Dean and Matty may be emailed directly

An excellent and individual site for swinging contacts.

http://www.grndlvl.demon.co.uk

The Desyre Foundation

The Desyre Foundation is a British, Midlands-based organisation founded in 1996 with the intention of becoming a focus for the UK BDSM community. Their site advertises the clubs they run, and serves as a general BDSM resource. This provides an excellent starting point for those who wish to enter this fascinating erotic world, but be warned; it is not for prudes. The bulk of the site slows it down and makes navigation and readability less than perfect. The style is open and informative, with just a touch of megalomania for added interest.

Note: The Desyre Foundation is for consenting adults. Always respect other people's right to private space and personal choice. At clubs, follow dress-codes or you will not get in.

overall rating:
★★★★★
classification:
resource and club
updated:
frequently
navigation:
★★★★
content:
★★★★★
readability:
★★★★
orgasm rating:
not applicable
orgasm rating:
not applicable
speed:
★★★★
UK

SPECIAL FEATURES

Membership Desyre Foundation Membership is only open to UK residents. With it comes a fortnightly newsletter, information on parties, events and contacts, support and discounts for their events, and the products listed in their catalogue of clothing and sex toys.

Republique is the Desyre Foundation's Stoke-on-Trent Club. A monthly event with a strict fetish dress code, running from 9pm until 2am, it is open to non-members, and all the details you could possibly need are provided on the site. The club includes a market area and a customised dungeon, while food is available.

The Bridge is the Birmingham club, run along identical lines but on a different night.

Desyre Gallery shows photos of genuine scenes from the clubs, including a girl about to be spanked, another girl tied by her grinning Master, and a third naked in dog's collar and chain. The club is run by a male dominant, which perhaps accounts for the selection of photos which perhaps misrepresents the less specialist atmosphere of the club. We liked them anyway, but remember, whether you're titillated or shocked by such scenes, they are consensual acts between informed, intelligent adults.

Desyre Links Extensive, categorised links to other UK BDSM sites. Useful, if not quite comprehensive, with information on everything from sexual politics to hot wax play technique.

Fetish-Net UK is a more general BDSM resource site run by the same people.

OTHER FEATURES

News, information and the Desyre Foundation's product catalogue are also offered.

A great resource for the British BDSM community, especially in the Midlands.

http://www.torturegarden.com

Torture Garden

Torture Garden is the UK's second senior fetish club and the perfect entry point for anyone interested in alternative sexual sub-culture. Founded in 1990, the club now regularly attracts over 1,000 people. The style is broad, and completely open, embracing everybody but the boring. It focuses on fetishism, tattoos, piercing and connected elements of fashion, cabaret, and performance art. Torture Garden can be the perfect meeting place for the sexually liberated. It is designed for people of all ages and sexual orientations, although the trend is towards the young and fashionable. For the first timer, just walking into Torture Garden can be a really powerful experience, try it!

Note: Torture Garden is not a brothel; respect other peoples' right to private space and personal choice. Follow dress-codes or you will not get in.

overall rating:
★★★★★
classification:
club
updated:
frequently
navigation:
★★★★
content:
★★★★★
readability:
★★★★
orgasm rating:
not applicable
orgasm rating:
not applicable
speed:
★★★
US

SPECIAL FEATURES

Torture Garden is the main club, with information posted on forthcoming events, the club ethos and history, illustrated with pictures from among the more spectacular club goers. Torture Garden is not for the faint hearted, nor for those just after easy sex, but it provides a door to a world of erotic experience.

Seed is a non-fetish cyber dance club from the same people, trendy, alternative but less fantastic.

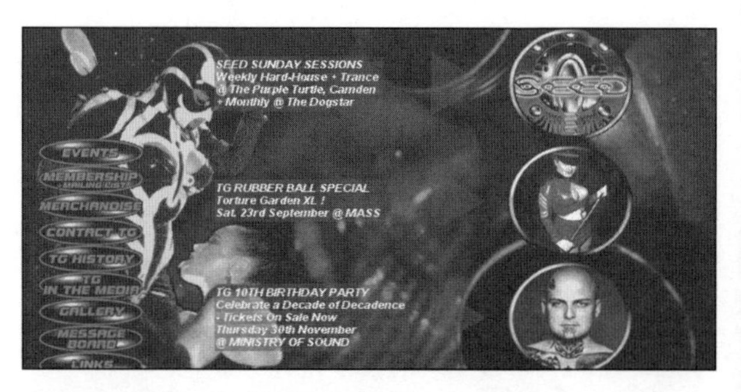

Ad Nauseam is a Torture Garden offshoot focussing on bizarre cabaret and exotic music.

Club Flesh is the section for serious fetishists, with a slant towards classic erotic style.

OTHER FEATURES

Membership and ticket information are provided. Torture Garden books and videos are available for sale.

A great club for alternative sexual lifestyles.

http://www.adultfriendfinder.com

Adult Friend Finder

Adult Friend Finder is a US-based but international contact service for adults. They claim a membership of over five million, with another 10,000 joining each day. The basic service is free, but to use the site efficiently you need one of the two paid services available, silver and gold, costing $79.95 and $99.95 a year respectively. Registration is entirely free, and we found them refreshingly open-minded, offering contacts not just between heterosexual women and men, but also for gay men, lesbians, couples seeking a third party, and groups. Members can also list sexual interests, including cross dressing, BDSM, exhibitionism and other alternative activities. Data may be accessed by region, including the UK and just about every other country. The site is reasonably fast and easy to navigate, adding to what we felt to be a top-quality contact service.

overall rating:
★★★★
classification:
contacts
updated:
constantly
navigation:
★★★★
content:
★★★★★
readability:
★★★★
orgasm rating:
not applicable
orgasm rating:
not applicable
speed:
★★★★
US R £

SPECIAL FEATURES

Basic membership is the free service, allowing you to add your profile to the database and view three profiles each day. Your profile can be edited and a photo added and changed at will, but you cannot see other members' photos. You can receive emails and send one every day as well as access the Hot List facility, which allows you to keep track of members you are interested in. The database may be searched by handle. The majority of chatrooms are open to you.

Silver Membership is a greatly improved service, with no limit on emails sent or received. Other members' photos are available for viewing, and you get lists of members whom you may be interested in. The database may be searched according to standard criteria. All chatrooms are accessible. You are also provided with technical support by the site, and there are no banner ads.

Gold Membership is the top service, guaranteeing your details at the top of each list, which apparently creates five times as many views by others. Details of new members in whom you might be interested are emailed to you (via the Cupid service). The database may be searched in detail. All chatrooms are accessible. You receive priority technical support.

OTHER FEATURES

Adult Friend Finder also offers a list of answers to frequently asked questions, and welcomes feedback. A shop is also offered, along with a magazine with a large choice of articles.

An impressively large and cosmopolitan contact site.

http://www.swapscene.com/search/av/UKsexcontacts.html

Emma & Carl's UK-Swapscene

overall rating:
★★★★
classification:
contacts
updated:
constantly
navigation:
★★★★
content:
★★★★★
readability:
★★★
orgasm rating:
not applicable
orgasm rating:
not applicable
speed:
★★★
UK R £

Carl and Emma's is a swingers' website, not a dating agency, and surfers should be aware that, by and large, the site is designed for getting people together for sexual encounters. The site is UK-only and includes several thousand members. Membership costs £20 for a year or £12 for six months, which we feel is good value. The style of the site is personal and enthusiastic, being a genuine swingers' resource rather than merely an attempt to make money. We found the presentation unnecessarily fancy and rather hard to follow, as well as being slow, but the content is everything swingers could wish for.

Note: The swinging scene is for consenting adults to get together and have fun. Abuse the system and you won't get any!

SPECIAL FEATURES

Place Advert This is a free facility for couples and single females, enabling a detailed ad to be placed. Members can then reply to you even if you are not a member yourself. Single males can only place ads if they are members, which is a sensible way of reducing that perennial problem of swinging, the excess of single males.

Parties and Meets lists swinging events around the country along with all necessary details.

Live Chat is a free facility.

Contact Adverts is the heart of the site, with adverts from those seeking swinging partners. These are initially divided into Males Seeking, Females Seeking, and Couples Seeking. Click on your choice and you go to a list of ads with basic criteria: location, who you want to meet, whether a photo has been posted, and a reference number. Click on what you fancy and you go to a detailed ad, to which members can respond. We had a look at a charming young couple from Southampton who were seeking other couples and single females in order to develop social as well as sexual friendships.

Members Galleries features pictures of members in thumbnailed galleries, and all are more or less titillating. Each picture will take you to the member's ad, which makes it an efficient browsing resource.

Resources features articles, information, listings, adult jokes, anything relevant to the subject.

Star Advert is a featured ad, rotated weekly.

OTHER FEATURES

The site also offers links, help, a message board, and an opportunity to report obsolete adverts.

A great facility for the UK swinging scene.

http://www.glassbar.ndo.co.uk

The Glass Bar

overall rating:
★★★★
classification:
club
updated:
monthly
navigation:
★★★★
content:
★★★
readability:
★★★★
orgasm rating:
not applicable
orgasm rating:
not applicable
speed:
★★★★★
UK

The Glass Bar advertises itself as 'London's sole women-only space that is non-scene, empty of screaming queens, gay boy drama, devoid of Soho-hyped attitude, friendly approachable bar staff, and gives you change out of a round.' (Presumably they don't really mean they're devoid of friendly approachable bar staff.) It is a women-only private members' club rather than a lesbian bar, and the only criterion for joining is that you must be female. The site advertises the bar and is straightforward and easy to navigate, although perhaps there could have been a bit more content. The titles on the mini jumpstation at the bottom of each page are not immediately clear.

SPECIAL FEATURES

Activities gives a full monthly calendar of Glass Bar events. The bar is closed on Mondays and there are various weekly and monthly activities.

Relax features the bar's details and policy. It can be booked for special events or private viewings of artwork, but is primarily designed as a comfortable, stress-free meeting place for women. Sofas are provided for visitors to cuddle, but only cuddle.

Dine is a link to the related Therapy Restaurant.

Hot Links seemed like a bit of an exaggeration when we visited, as it covered only the women's sex shop, Sh!, and sites for transport in London.

Venues gives the addresses of the Glass Bar, Therapy and two other planned venues with similar styles.

OTHER FEATURES

The Glass Bar can be emailed and encourages feedback. There is also a fun page planned.

The supporting site for the Glass Bar, a women only bar in London.

http://www.outpersonals.com

OutPersonals.com

OutPersonal.com is a similar site to Adult Friend Finder, but exclusively for gay men. Basic membership is free after the completion of a detailed questionnaire, including information on languages and basic sexual preferences. Much better services are available for those with Silver and Gold membership, which cost $89.96 a year and $119.96 a year respectively. This is a commercial service, with an impersonal style, but it is large, and covers the entire world. The presentation is detailed, though it is fussy, with rather small fonts, but it is clear enough, with few banners. The search system is good, allowing for detailed searches, although with limited reference to specific sexual preferences.

overall rating:
★★★★
classification:
contacts
updated:
constantly
navigation:
★★★★
content:
★★★
readability:
★★★★
orgasm rating:
not applicable
orgasm rating:
not applicable
speed:
★★★
US £ R

SPECIAL FEATURES

Help is a major feature with a large FAQ section covering everything you need to know about the site. A feedback form is provided for more detailed questions, which we tested and found extremely efficient.

Members' Facilities Outpersonal members receive a basic service, including the creation of a personal profile, access to chatrooms, a personal hotlist of favourite members, database search for members by handle, uploading and changing of a personal photo, personality tests, and a voice greeting facility. Each day ten personal profiles of other members can be viewed (but not their photos) and two emails sent. Basic technical support is provided. The erotic gallery may be viewed at thumbnail level.

Silver Membership allows unlimited emailing, viewing of other members' photos, a standard database search, your handle listed on the recent members' list, and faster technical support. The erotic gallery may be viewed in full size.

Gold Membership gives all the privileges of Silver Membership, plus a priority search facility, a guarantee of being placed at the top of each search list and, improved technical support. Most importantly, you may use the Love Dog service, which will automatically email you the details of all new members with compatible profiles. Gold members may turn the banner advertising off.

OTHER FEATURES

The site also offers links to other contact sites, and a large magazine covering gay men's issues. Several other features are available to members, including chat and an erotic gallery with over 500 pictures.

A big, commercial contact site.

http://www.ronstorme.com

Ron Storme's Club Travestie

This is the promotional site for Ron Storme's, London's premier transvestite club. The club was founded in 1980 and has built up a unique atmosphere of sexy, sleazy chic. It is welcoming to everyone into cross-dressing, from professional drag queens to bricklayers in floral frocks, from outrageous gay transvestites in gold lamé to straight guys who like to dress up in their wife's undies now and then. Women are welcome too. Like the club, the site is open and relaxed, with no hint of the insecurities and doubts that so often go with this subject. The layout is simple, with easy navigation, and no adverts or distractions, though more information would have been helpful for newcomers.

overall rating:
★★★★
classification:
specialist service
updated:
monthly
navigation:
★★★★★
content:
★★★
readability:
★★★★★
orgasm rating:
not applicable
orgasm rating:
not applicable
speed:
★★★★
UK

SPECIAL FEATURES

Coming Events provides information on coming club events, laid on month by month. Generally these are at Stepney's, an East End Club on the Commercial Road. The club runs every Saturday from 9pm until 2.30am, with tickets available on the door at £5. Along with low bar prices, this must make it one of the best value clubs in London. Each night is themed, and some include cabaret acts.

Photos shows galleries of past events at the club and photos of some of the more spectacular costumes worn over the years. The sense of over-the-top glamour comes across, but to really appreciate the club you need to visit.

OTHER FEATURES
The site can be contacted, and there is a notice board, but it has been created purely to promote the club, without links or other support features.

The site for London's top transvestite club.

http://www.webwiz.net.clients.htm

Web Connect Internet Personals

Web Connect claims to be the world's largest internet personals service, with some 3,000 matches made every day. The site can be accessed for free, and ads placed for free, but in order to respond to ads, you need to become an AYCE (All You Can Email) member. This costs from between $24.95 per month to $99.95 for a year, which isn't particularly good value. On entering the site you are passed to the one-and-only database, of which WebConnect is a member. This is huge and worldwide; a simple system that allows you to access information according to a rather limited set of criteria. Men and women may state a preference for men, women, pen pals, or the disabled. There is no facility for couples, groups, or any but basic sexual preferences. The site is easy to read and navigate, and fast enough, but only suitable for straightforward one-to-one contact.

overall rating:
★★★
classification:
contacts
updated:
constantly
navigation:
★★★★
content:
★★★
readability:
★★★★
orgasm rating:
not applicable
orgasm rating:
not applicable
speed:
★★★★
US £ R

SPECIAL FEATURES

There are three ways to find someone among the Internet Personals ads:

Browse The Ads The basic option that allows you to surf their ads according to major factors like geographical location. We had a look for women's ads in the London area. Fifty were listed, the majority with a photo. Click on each and you go to the full ad, which describes the person and their lifestyle. If you want to reply you must join AYCE.

Find a Match A more precise option, allowing you to cut your ads down by not only geographic location, but age, physical characteristics and lifestyle. You may also cut out all those which do not include photos. We were impressed by the system's ability to find obscure matches in obscure places, but there is no facility for finding a partner according to mutual sexual preferences.

Mailbox Search A chance to return to specific ads by their mailbox number, assuming you noted it down the first time around!

OTHER FEATURES

The site also provides tips on writing your ad, and general help and information on the service.

A huge but simple dating site. Great for dating, poor for sexy encounters.

Section 10

something different

We have chosen to define the term 'fetish' broadly, taking into account everything that places an erotic focus on a particular behaviour, object, or part of the body other than the main erogenous zones. Basic obsessions, such as breasts, we have not included, nor the commonest ones, such as girls' underwear. We have also tried to concentrate on British sites and favourite British kinks. No UK survey of fetish sex would be complete without mentioning spanking. We have avoided extreme forms of sadomasochism, bondage, and anything blatantly illegal, and anything that pushes the boundaries of consent.

With fetishism, and in particular with acts that involve one participant's surrender of control to another, it is easy to forget that these are voluntary acts. Ultimately, it must always be the submissive partner who is in control and who sets the limits on what is acceptable and what is not. Fetish sites often make this clear. Sometimes they do not, preferring to present the fetish as a fantasy. For instance, a spanking photoset may appear to show a woman being coerced into accepting corporal punishment, often from somebody with authority over her. In reality she is a paid model and almost always a genuine enthusiast who enjoys being spanked and doesn't mind doing it for commercial purposes. Much of the professional UK spanking scene is controlled by women, and ads for models bring a plentiful response. The same is true for other fetishes which involve taking sexual control over another person.

The keywords for fetish sex are Safe, Sane, and Consensual:

Safe Take care to avoid anything that risks transmission of disease or lasting damage. Always sterilise equipment that is to be inserted into body cavities or when there is a risk of exchange of body fluids. Always test bondage equipment for strength before use. Get to know someone before you play. Don't go home with strangers, or at the very least make sure somebody knows where you are and that the person you are going with knows this too.

Sane Take care of your playmate's mental health, because even light bondage can be an extraordinarily powerful experience, especially for beginners. Always use a stop word and never ignore it. Green for go, Amber for slow and Red for STOP NOW are simple and effective. Being dominant does not make you an expert – learn your skills from someone more experienced.

Consensual Fetish sex play is for informed, consenting adults. Talk before you play, discuss limits and remember that being in control during play does not give you the right to control in normal life. Permission given under duress is not consent. By definition, nobody can give consent until they reach the age of consent.

Having said all that, it's supposed to be fun. If it's not then you're not doing it properly, on the net or in reality.

http://fetish.erosvillage/beartickler

Bear's Tickling Fantasies

Bear's Tickling Fantasies is an excellent site not only for those who love the idea of being tickled or tickling others, but for erotic bondage, foot fetishism, and other related kinks. To anyone who just enjoys straight sex this may all seem a bit obscure, but there is plenty of nudity thrown in and a visit to the site should prove amusing at the very least. There are a few advertising banners, including one or two designed to be misleading, but the site is still reasonably easy to navigate, readable, and reasonably fast. The style is personal and fun; very much like tickling, really. We had some difficulty with the URL, but access can be gained through Webring and then the Erotic Tickling Webring.

overall rating:
★★★★★
classification:
homepage
updated:
frequently
navigation:
★★★★
content:
★★★★★
readability:
★★★★
orgasm rating:
♀♀♀♀
orgasm rating:
♂♂♂♂
speed:
★★★★
US

SPECIAL FEATURES

A clear, well-designed jumpstation at the bottom of the main page gives access to all areas of the site.

Photo Galleries are presented in five main areas: Tickled Men, Bondage, Inquisition, Tickled Fems, and Nylon Tickling. Both Tickled Men and Tickled Fems lead to several large, thumbnailed galleries showing in all several hundred pictures of people being tickled. There is also a lot of bondage, with the majority of scenes involving the helpless victim being tickled on the feet or under the arms while tied in some vulnerable position. Others showed more intimate or directly sexual tickling. Bondage is just that, while Inquisition scenes are those in which the victim might be being tickled in an effort to extract information from her or him. Nylon Tickling covers girls being tickled through their stockings or tights, and often tied up as well.

Tickle Art contains four galleries of tickling art, some good, some poor, some humorous, some erotic.

Stories features a selection of erotic tickling stories. We took a look at Greedy, which is fairly typical US college porn, with two nerds catching a popular girl by a trick, and tickling her. Soft, fun, and sexy, if not exactly literature.

Private is the private tickling gallery from the Bear and Holly, the site's host and hostess.

WAVS Tickling sound WAVs can be downloaded directly from the site.

OTHER FEATURES

The site provides extensive links, along with pages for news and video reviews. It is also a member of the Erotic Tickling Webring.

A great site for tickling fantasy, erotic bondage and more.

http:www.belly.co.uk

Belly Magazine – Where Fat Chicks Are Cool

overall rating:
★★★★★
classification:
ezine
updated:
occasionally
navigation:
★★★★
content:
★★★★★
readability:
★★★★
orgasm rating:
♀♀
orgasm rating:
♂♂♂
speed:
★★★★
UK

Do you ever feel overweight? Take a look at Belly and all such illusions will be dispelled. We had to give this site five stars for sheer audacity. In a world where women are made to feel ashamed unless they look like skeletons, where having a 'big bottom' is cause for blushing embarrassment, Belly gives us huge, beautiful women presented naked and proud. It is specialist, no doubt, so we couldn't give it a spectacular orgasm rating, but we really liked the upbeat, playful style. The site is simple, fast, and easy to follow, with only a little advertising.

SPECIAL FEATURES

Issue #4 is the latest issue of Belly. This contains three photo features, fiction, letters, amateur photos, and personals. On the site there are sample pictures from the photo features, including a huge yet shapely bottom being painted with liquid latex. The issue's special feature is on the delights of feeding, complete with a girl whose fantasy is to be fed and fed and fed!

Galleries shows photos from this issue and previous issues, all of big women, and photographed in the variety of locations and poses you might expect of a mainstream sex magazine. When Belly says big women, they don't mean slightly plump.

Personals is an extensive feature, making this site a worthwhile contact site as well as an ezine. This is a voicemail dating system with all the necessary details presented on the top page. When we visited, there were ads from 56 women seeking men, 17 men seeking women, four women seeking other women, and eight others with less common needs. From the way fat people are portrayed in the media, you would expect the ads to be from desperate women seeking long term partners. More typical of these ads, however, is Laura, who was advertising to have two blacks guys at the same time.

Modelling Belly is always keen for new models, and the magazine can be contacted by anyone interested.

OTHER FEATURES

Links are currently a minor feature, but an expansion is planned. The hard copy magazine can be purchased online.

The ezine for big, beautiful women.

http://hades.nixnet.com

Mistress Hades

Mistress Hades is a wonderful hotchpoch of a site, designed to delight the fetishist and fascinate others. It is female-run and primarily designed for a female audience, but both sexes should enjoy it so long as they know what to expect.

overall rating:
★★★★★
classification:
homepage
updated:
variably
navigation:
★★★★
content:
★★★★★
readability:
★★★★
orgasm rating:
♀♀♀♀
orgasm rating:
♂♂♂♂
speed:
★★★★
UK

SPECIAL FEATURES

Mistress Hades is about the Mistress, her personal philosophy, and the rules under which she dominates her slave boys.

London Fetish Fair is a monthly market run by Mistress Hades and promoted from this website. The fair is a collection of individual stalls at which any erotic goods can be purchased or ordered, a social event and an entry point for anybody interested in the fetish scene.

Birch Bottoms and Lovitt Pony-girl Club A speciality of the hostess, with a female submissive orientation. Pony-girls and boys, a piggy-girl, and a zebra-girl are presented on these pages.

OTHER FEATURES

Stories, links, news, novels, and contacts are offered, and there are lists of alphabetical spanking and bondage; an attempt by the Mistress to spank her way through the alphabet of people.

A great site, with something for everyone into fetishes.

overall rating:
★★★★★
classification:
specialist service
updated:
frequently
navigation:
★★★
content:
★★★★★
readability:
★★★★
orgasm rating:
♀♀♀
orgasm rating:
♂♂♂♂
speed:
★★★★
US

http://www.patches.net

Patches' Place

Patches Place is probably the oldest and most fully developed watersports resource on the net. The site is free and covers anything and everything to do with girls peeing. Although aimed mainly at heterosexual men, anyone into this fetish should have this bookmarked. The style is jokey and the presentation a bit cluttered, making it hard to navigate at times, but there is no shortage of content. Although free of banners and pop-ups, there are recommendations for related paysites sprinkled throughout the text. The speed is fair and the jumpstation clear. Patches' Place is also a firm supporter of sexual freedom on the net for consenting adults, and even presents a link to their attorneys on the main page.

SPECIAL FEATURES

Links is the main feature of the site; a constantly updated listing of links to other watersports sites. Some will simply take you to a single watersports picture; others to large gallery sites. Updates of established sites are also included, along with permanent links to other major watersports sites. When we visited, there were five pages of links, but inevitably this includes those that quickly disappear or change. We looked at Female Desperation; a large, free gallery site dedicated to women getting caught short in awkward places.

Videos is the feature that supports the site, offering a huge list of watersports videos for sale which are mainly their own. There were over 100 titles available when we visited, covering just about every aspect of the fetish imaginable.

Gallery is Patches' own gallery of watersports pics, mainly video captures. These will not display on older browsers. We took a look at the clearly named Wet Panty Girls set, which had a deliciously naughty feel to it, although the picture quality could have been better.

Stories is a large collection of stories centred on peeing. These are mainly amateur and vary greatly in quality, although with so many listed, everyone ought to be able to find something to keep them happy. Related links are also provided.

Books is a listing of books with watersports content, set out by author.

OTHER FEATURES

Patches' Place also includes an FAQ section, news, humor, personals, IRC chat, information on rights, and general watersports information.

The net's top watersports resource, and they don't mean canoeing. Strictly specialist.

overall rating:	★★★★★
classification:	homepage
updated:	frequently
navigation:	★★★★★
content:	★★★★★
readability:	★★★★
orgasm rating:	♀♀♀♀
orgasm rating:	♂♂♂
speed:	★★★★
UK	

http://www.ranch.demon.co.uk

Pony Girl UK

We chose this site as the best of those devoted to this unusual, but increasingly popular fetish. Pony Girl UK is a free and very genuine site, run by a female enthusiast. As she explains, pony-girl play is one of a group of principally female fetishes involving animal imagery in fantasy role play. Others we have met include puppy-girls, piggy-girls, and even zebra-girls. It has nothing whatever to do with bestiality. Pony-girl play is no simple fantasy, but combines elements of submission, exhibitionism, bondage, light corporal punishment, and more, making it perhaps the most elaborate and subtle of all fetishes. The site is also well designed, very easy to navigate, and pretty fast.

SPECIAL FEATURES

About This Site is an introduction to the site and hostess.

Stories features one story of the hostess' own, and recommendations for books devoted to the subject. A wide if not comprehensive range.

What Is a Pony-girl? A detailed explanation of the fetish as BDSM role play. This is from a personal point of view, and some will doubtless be left bemused, but it was nevertheless a good introduction. Essentially, anything a real pony can do a pony-girl should be able to do, from simply being naked in a harness to dressage or pulling a buggy. She also explains that this is a genuine erotic pleasure in itself and not merely an excuse for easy sex – a fact that is often missed in explorations of fetishism.

Links gives you an extensive list of links to other pony-play sites, including groups and suppliers of tack. Tawsingham is included, which is probably the UK's biggest pony-play club. Again, not quite comprehensive.

Pictures There are currently 14 categorised galleries, with more to come. We have seen pony-play pictures not included in these galleries, but very few! We took a look at the Posing Pony section to discover 22 pictures of girls in bridles and harnesses; some even with tails. It's strange, it's specialist, it certainly won't be to everyone's taste, but we loved it.

OTHER FEATURES

There is also a chance to comment on and provide feedback to the site, along with general information.

A delightful site exploring the world of pony-girl play.

overall rating:
★★★★★
classification:
homepage
updated:
weekly
navigation:
★★★★★
content:
★★★★★
readability:
★★★★★
orgasm rating:
♀♀♀♀♀
orgasm rating:
♂♂♂♂♂
speed:
★★★
NL

http://www.wulfram.net

Wulfram's Homepage

If the erotic spanking of females is your thing, then this is a must. Otherwise, it is not for you. Wulfram is a genuine enthusiast and has created a site appealing to both male and female spanking fetishists. It is free, user-friendly, and welcoming, with none of the misogyny or aggression that often comes with SM-oriented sites. The content is mixed, with pictures, stories, and chat, all designed to appeal to the chosen audience. Visitor participation is encouraged, and not just with the chatrooms; requests are considered and opinions listened to. Wulfram understands erotic spanking, and ultimately this is what makes the site worthy of its five-star rating.

SPECIAL FEATURES

Picture galleries These are extensive, and a new one is added about once a week. They are well presented and easily navigable, though the file size can be unwieldy. The content is largely drawn from magazines and videos, with some amateur input. There are several categories, each devoted to an aspect of spanking fantasy. The main galleries show classic, carefully selected spanking sequences, with pictures from across the web. Spankables is what it says; pictures of beautiful women the viewer would wish to spank, suitably posed. The cartoon gallery covers work by artists such as Paula Meadows. Requests covers sequences visitors have asked to see, while the White Panties Spanking Club covers a favourite topic.

Movie Projects These are often large-scale video pieces taken from classics such as Little Red Apples. Inevitably slow, but a must for those who like to see it actually happen. RealPlayer is needed to view these and can be downloaded from the site. First timers may need a little practice.

Story collections Extensive collections are featured from various writers, notably Daria Little. These are well enough written, and again show genuine enthusiasm, although they show less variety than they might.

Chatrooms Several of these are offered, two of which appear to be particularly busy. Visitors are offered the chance to add their own room.

OTHER FEATURES

Links, resources and update listings are offered, as well as credits, which is unusual. There is also a touch of humour, with spanking cartoons and their captions translated into a multitude of languages.

The site for lovers of female submissive spanking. Friendly, enthusiastic, and genuine.

overall rating:
★★★★
classification:
specialist service
updated:
biweekly
navigation:
★★★★★
content:
★★★★★
readability:
★★★★★
orgasm rating:
♀♀
orgasm rating:
♂♂♂♂
speed:
★★★★
FR

http://www.aragornsfeetlinks.com

Aragorn's Feetlinks

The internet is full of sites devoted to women's legs, feet, and footwear; so much so that it proved near impossible to choose one site over another. We finally chose Aragorn's Feetlinks for its sheer, obsessive eagerness and because from the site it is possible to reach everything anybody could possibly want on this topic. It is mainly a links site, with a small gallery section. The site design is simple and efficient, with a good balance of art and function and no distracting banners at all. From the mainpage the surfer may chose either English or French versions of the site.

SPECIAL FEATURES

Welcome covers updates, revisions and links to top listings for heels, feet, and hose.

Links is the heart of the site, divided into 62 areas when we visited. These include sites listed by different languages, but are mainly divided by specific fetish preference, from the obvious (high heels, boots and such), to the not so obvious (long toenails, dangling feet, dirty feet, even used shoes). A look at High Heels Fetish revealed 164 separate sites, each briefly described, including such information as whether it is a paysite or requires AVS. Toe Cleavage Pumps anyone? Even Long Toenails covered 19 sites. It would be a very particular foot fetishist indeed who couldn't find what they wanted.

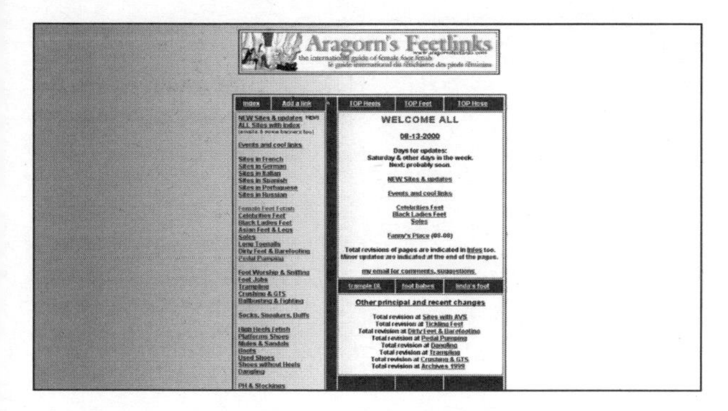

Fanny's Place is the personal gallery of the host's wife, Fanny, a woman with beautiful, elegant legs and feet, which is just as well, really.

OTHER FEATURES

The site may be contacted and relevant links sent in.

The perfect bookmark for lovers of women's legs, feet, and footwear.

overall rating:
★★★★
classification:
homepage
updated:
variably
navigation:
★★★
content:
★★★★
readability:
★★★★
orgasm rating:
♀♀♀♀♀
orgasm rating:
♂♂♂♂♂
speed:
★★★★
UK

http://www.bdsmcafe.com

B & belle

B & belle is a set of related homepages hosted by a couple who met on the web. The content is unashamedly sadomasochistic, and while presented in a friendly, fun way, it is not for the uninitiated. Pictures, stories, and comments are provided, covering topics ranging from spanking and mindplay to heavy bondage and sexual torture. These are split into seven different zones, which have considerable overlap and can be confusing. Everything is free, although they do host the BDSM Planet paysite as well. There are commercial banners and leads, but not so many as to destroy the pleasure of the site. The need for consent and care is stressed, and B & belle clearly know what they are doing, making the site a useful resource for budding sadomasochists of both sexes.

SPECIAL FEATURES

BDSM Café is the heart of the site, with listings of stories, pictures, and information covering spanking and bondage, along with more extreme erotic tortures such as nipple clamping and hot wax treatment. There are sections on male and female domination, erotic cartoons and art, a tribute to Betty Page, and a little gay BDSM. Some of these are straightforward galleries, while some lead to other sites, which can be irritating.

BDSM Palace is a similar site with different galleries and story collections, and even erotic poetry.

Bondage Basement is another similar site, but with an emphasis on bondage.

Pornoprose Magazine An ezine, again with similar content, but less emphasis on BDSM. Straight, gay, and lesbian topics are mixed with B & belle's happy acceptance of all tastes and sexualities.

Torture Zone is the section leading to the Pornoprose page.

Bi-Curious This section is dedicated to those wishing to experiment with bisexuality (both male and female). A useful resource for those who are uncertain or simply wish to experiment, both for straight and kinky bisexuality.

Belle's Bottom is a picture site which is updated daily, and is fast and easy to use, with the emphasis on spanking pictures.

OTHER FEATURES

Links, fetish resources, ecards and personals are all available from these sites.

A great site for sadomasochists. A little muddled maybe, but you can feel the enthusiasm!

overall rating:
★★★★
classification:
specialist service
updated:
frequently
navigation:
★★★
content:
★★★★
readability:
★★★
orgasm rating:
♀♀♀
orgasm rating:
♂♂♂♂
speed:
★★★
US

http://www.malesubmission.com

Celebrate Male Submission

Celebrate Male Submission promotes itself as the first true resource site for the male submissive. Certainly there is no shortage of information on the topic, although as an American site some areas will be less useful to British surfers. The site is genuine and helpful, while many sites aimed at sexually submissive men are exploitative. If anything, the style is too enthusiastic, with too much information presented too fast. Nevertheless, if you are prepared to dig a little it does form a valuable resource and a good start point. It is a free site supported by advertising banners, but these are less intrusive than in many sites. As any site of this sort should, it stresses that the content is aimed at consenting, informed adults.

SPECIAL FEATURES

The welcome page lists twenty-seven features. Somewhat overwhelmed, we took a look at those we felt surfers would most like to visit.

Mission Statement this rambles rather but essentially states that the hostess, Mistress Littlestar, intends to set up a site to provide a friendly web environment and resource for submissive males. In thise she has undoubtedly succeeded.

Showcases features original images of males submission. The majority of these show the hostess dominating men. Guest photos are also included, and there should be enough to keep the most demanding of male subs happy.

Male FAQ's Questions and answers for the guidance of male submissives. As it is a topic about which many feel insecure, we decided to take a detailed look at this area. Twenty-six articles are presented, starting with basics such as What is Submission? and leading up to advanced topics such as The ins and Outs of Cock and Ball Torture. The advice is intelligent and shows considerable experience. It is also less hidebound than much similar advice, and admits that females can also be submissive if not that many men happily enjoy both roles.

OTHER FEATURES

Features also include an area for dominant women, extensive links, a what's new feature, stories, events, opinions from both dominant women and submissive men, a contact service and listings for dominant women.

A good resource for male submissives. Focused on the US.

overall rating:
★★★★
classification:
specialist service
updated:
occasionally
navigation:
★★★
content:
★★★★
readability:
★★★★
orgasm rating:
♀♀♀♀
orgasm rating:
♂♂♂
speed:
★★★★
UK

http://www.the-firm.org

The Firm

The firm is the brainchild of the inimitable Ishmael Skyes, and describes itself as a Secret Politico-Criminal Organisation. Founded in 1988, the Firm is senior to just about every other UK fetish organisation. The website may be treated as a fetish resource. The contents are varied and idiosyncratic, but relate to various aspects of fetishism with an emphasis on male submission and female erotic boxing. It is free and uncluttered by banners, if sometimes hard to navigate.

SPECIAL FEATURES

About the Firm is a welcome page introducing the Firm.

Firm Events The Firm runs three fetish events as well as private parties. Neverwhere is monthly, while the Pleasurezone is a bigger, annual event. The Boat, the annual fetishists' river outing on the Thames, is famous and justly so. The Firm also supplies support and manpower for other fetish organisations and sexual liberty groups.

The Next Party gives details of the next event.

Boxing is a speciality of the site, and features comments and pictures that deal with erotic female boxing. A large new gallery is promised.

Dominatrix Toxaemia Advice for dominant females, both novices and the experienced. This is presented as a pastiche, but the advice is still valuable as Ishmael, one of the fetish scene's most experienced male submissives, does know what he is talking about.

Sad Sub Syndrome Advice for submissive men, again presented as a pastiche, but again worth paying attention to.

Publications This features Ishmael's books, both fiction and non-fiction. The novelettes are drawn from his experiences with the Muir Academy, an adult "school", and from his fertile imagination. Samples are presented. Of the others, Freewhealing: A Hitchhiker's Guide to the Scene is much the most valuable. This covers his own experiences as a novice in the then tiny UK fetish scene and provides invaluable advice to anyone interested in the realities of fetishism, particularly submissive men. Useful advice is also given on how to avoid being economically exploited. Quest is a sequel of sorts, and semi-autobiographical. It is a little abstract, but we were fascinated.

OTHER FEATURES

Links are also included, and a newsletter, along with a bio of Ishmael Skyes and information about the history of the Firm.

A useful fetish resource site.

overall rating:
★★★
classification:
homepage
updated:
occasionally
navigation:
★★★★
content:
★★★
readability:
★★★★★
orgasm rating:
♀♀♀
orgasm rating:
♂♂♂♂
speed:
★★★★
US

http://www.geocities.com/SouthBeach/Sands/9841

Fetish Girls

Mistress Claire is the hostess of Fetish Girls, a free site dedicated to women in rubber, PVC, and leather with an undercurrent of female domination. The site is entered through a couple of introductory pages showing Mistress Claire herself, a cheerfully pretty young woman who doesn't look as if she'd hurt a fly. Could the site be fake? Probably not, or there'd be more banners, but it's good anyway. Essentially Fetish Girls is a straight forward gallery site, but the reasonable speed, easy access, and lack of banners make it worthwhile, as does the personal style. We did feel that there could be a lot more to it, but it was still well worth a visit.

SPECIAL FEATURES

Fetish girls lists ten galleries leading from two pages. Each gallery contains a dozen or so pictures. These are specialist, with little nudity, but should appeal equally to those with a penchant for rubber, PVC, and leather. Anyone who enjoys the fantasy of being dominated by women in these exotic costumes, male or female, should also enjoy the site. Mistress Claire may state her preference for female domination, but the galleries also contain some very sexy female submissive imagery. Submissive men will enjoy shots such as the picture taken at kneeling level of two haughty young women clad from necks to fingers and toes in shiny rubber. Others might prefer the pretty, beautifully-posed girl in a tight-waisted black rubber one piece, yellow mac, and yellow thighboots. One or two of the pictures show couples in femdom scenarios, with both male and female submissives.

OTHER FEATURES

Link are provided to related sites, also a guestbook.

Straightforward but good homepage for images of women in rubber, PVC and leather.

Section 11

sexual politics

Despite gradual liberalisation of the UK's anti-sex laws, restrictive and repressive attitudes are still depressingly common. Many sexual freedom groups exist to counteract this, mainly from the strong gay and SM communities. We have chosen five sites to review, four of which are UK-based organisations that welcome members and support.

For the average heterosexual couple, fighting for sexual freedom may seem something of a storm in a tea cup. For gays and SMers this is not the case. In addition to broader rights issues, numerous people have been prosecuted over recent years for sexual acts taking place in private between consenting adults. Clubs and magazines have been forced to close down, even in cases where no charges were brought or when prosecutions have failed.

To take one example, Club Whiplash was raided in 1994 by over 60 police officers. Whiplash was a members' club devoted to consenting adult fetishists and never included paid sex in any form. The attempted prosecution of the owner fell through, costing the taxpayer several hundred thousand pounds for no gain to anybody.

http://www.outrage.cygnet.co.uk

Outrage!

overall rating:
★★★★★
classification:
specialist service
updated:
frequently
navigation:
★★★★
content:
★★★★★
readability:
★★★★★
orgasm rating:
not applicable
orgasm rating:
not applicable
speed:
★★★
UK

Outrage! describes itself as a broad-based group of queers committed to radical, non-violent direct action and civil disobedience. Their stated aims are to assert the dignity and human rights of queers; to fight homophobia, discrimination, and violence directed against homosexuals and to affirm the right of homosexuals to sexual freedom, choice, and self-determination. The site is free of adverts and is clearly set out, allowing surfers to choose from the extensive list of topics displayed on the site map. It is a little slow, but there is no doubt that if you want information on the recent history of sexual freedom campaigning in the UK you are almost certain to find it here. Within the site, jumpstations at the top of each main page allow quick access to those areas discussed below, some of the pages being very long.

SPECIAL FEATURES

The site opens with a list of text links to areas dealing with recent important issues, such as the trial of nailbomber David Copeland. Below are the group's aims and information on joining the campaign, making donations, and obtaining regular information updates by email.

Site Map is an enormous list of links presented as a scrollable frame. These include the main areas of the site and news dating back to the beginning of the 1990s. This makes it easy for you to keep up with current trends in the movement and search back for related news. News is divided into topical areas: Armed Forces, Commercial, Community, Education, Health, International, Media/Propaganda, Politics and Religion. We looked at the section on History, Ideas, and Activism, which explains the dedication of Outrage! to direct, non-violent action and covers their past successes and interaction with other homosexual rights groups. There is also an appeal for financial support, the group being run entirely by unpaid volunteers on a fraction of the budget of other groups with similar profiles. The Queer Intelligence Service gives press releases, recent and from earlier years, along with pictures of the some of the group's protests.

OTHER FEATURES

Outrage! also provides advice and support to homosexuals. The site lists links to related sites.

The site for the UK's longest-running direct action homosexual rights group.

http://www.fiawol.demon.co.uk/FAC

Feminists Against Censorship

This is the site of feminist pressure group, Feminists Against Censorship. Founded in 1989 to protest against the censorship of sexual media, FAC stands against the idea that feminism is inherently anti-pornography. FAC is a women's group opposed to all forms of sexual censorship of behaviour, imagery, and information. They support the rights of people to see what they please and do as they please. The site is simple, easy to use and practical in design. The style is forthright and clear, providing extensive information on censorship in the UK. If you oppose the censorship of sexual images, on the internet in particular, this is a useful group for men or women to be involved with.

SPECIAL FEATURES

FAQ provides answers to the main questions the group addresses. This covers their history and principles. Support for the group is entirely by donation. FAC is a voluntary, unpaid group. Men may join, but may not be members of the decision-making executive.

Publications is a list of books published by members of the group, covering the debate on pornography and censorship in detail. Come Quietly, to be published shortly, will deal with the issue of sex on the net, amongst others. Books cannot be ordered directly from the site, but in some cases links are provided for those who wish to order.

overall rating:
★★★★
classification:
specialist service
updated:
occasionally
navigation:
★★★★★
content:
★★★★
readability:
★★★★
orgasm rating:
not applicable
orgasm rating:
not applicable
speed:
★★★★
UK

Events FAC occasionally hold events to raise funds and heighten awareness of sexual issues. These can be among the best erotic events in the country, although when we visited nothing was planned for the immediate future.

Censorship Alert is the largest section of the site. This provides details of news on censorship and censorship related events. Topics such as government policy and European policy are dealt with, alongside smaller issues such as individual prosecutions under the UK pornography laws. An archive lists older news, and it is possible to register for notification of newly posted material.

OTHER FEATURES

FAC may be emailed, and links are provided to similar sites and for organisations with overlapping aims.

The site of a UK-based feminist anti-censorship pressure group.

http://www.sfc.org.uk

Sexual Freedom Coalition

The Sexual Freedom Coalition is a pressure group with a stated aim of 'Promoting reform of Britain's silly old sex laws'. The group was set up in 1996 following the forced cancellation of the 10th anniversary of the Sex Maniacs Ball and police raids on various sexually uninhibited clubs. The site is their presence on the web and provides not only their own platform but a useful resource for other UK sex related pressure groups. It is undoubtedly valuable, but as a site we found it cluttered and sometimes hard to follow.

overall rating:
★★★★
classification:
specialist service
updated:
occasionally
navigation:
★★★
content:
★★★★
readability:
★★★
orgasm rating:
not applicable
orgasm rating:
not applicable
speed:
★★★
UK

SPECIAL FEATURES

The opening page lists the group's aims and provides an introduction. SFC history and events are also covered, along with how to provide support and a list of associated organisations. Links lead to eight other areas of the site, including:

Press Releases and News covers the SFC's efforts to have the UK's sex laws changed and related news.

Consenting Adults Newspaper is an infrequent newspaper covering a broad variety of sex related issues but focusing on sex and the law.

Books and Videos A number of these are offered, mainly by Dr Tuppy Owens and related to issues of sexual politics and support for the sexually disadvantaged.

The Sex Maniacs Ball Reports and information on the annual event held in support of the Outsiders Group, a charity dedicated to sexual support and contact for the disabled.

The Erotic Awards is a list of individuals and organisations who have received awards for their sex related work from the Sex Maniacs Ball organisation.

Sexual Freedom Bill is a full and detailed list of the changes the SFC would like to see in UK law, designed to bring our laws into line with the European Union and to allow full freedom of sexual expression between consenting adults. This is extensive, ranging from a call for the abolition of the archaic Disorderly Houses Act of 1751 to demands for subtle changes in the wording of many modern bills.

OTHER FEATURES

Extensive links are provided, notably to the supporters of the SFC and to related groups such as the Spanner Trust.

The principal net resource for UK sex-related pressure groups.

http://www.stonewall.org.uk

Stonewall

overall rating:
★★★★
classification:
specialist service
updated:
frequently
navigation:
★★★★
content:
★★★★
readability:
★★★★★
orgasm rating:
not applicable
orgasm rating:
not applicable
speed:
★★★
UK

Stonewall is a civil rights group working for equality for lesbians, gay men and bisexuals. The site is designed to promote their interests on the internet and provide information on their campaigns. Currently the focus is on the repeal of Section 28, a piece of legislation preventing the promotion of lesbian and gay issues in schools. The site is well designed and clearly set out. The front page covers the group's basic program, with a jump station at the bottom for access to the more detailed areas of the site. We found some internal pages slow to load. The style is forthright and reasonable, the presentation easy to follow.

SPECIAL FEATURES

The main page covers the group's primary aim and immediate agenda, after which the site is divided into eight secondary areas:

General covers the background and aims of Stonewall in detail. Latest News announcements from the Stonewall Press Office and the archive of news material.

Stonewall Factsheets provides information about five key areas of their campaign, Gay Sex and the Law, Lesbian and Gay Parents, Public Opinion on Lesbian and Gay Rights, Same Sex Couples and Pension Schemes and Discrimination in the Workplace. The factsheets the most important current issues within these topics, such as the age of consent and the positions of gays within the armed forces. Books and information packs are also offered.

Immigration Group A support group specifically involved with the problems of lesbian and gay immigrants.

Parenting Group a group campaigning for equal rights for lesbian and gay children.

OTHER FEATURES

The remaining areas cover membership and support for Stonewall in the form of donations and feedback.

The site for the UK's largest gay rights group.

http://www.susiebright.com

Susie Bright

The website of Susie Bright, American columnist, sex writer and teacher. This is a large site, containing a huge volume of information about the writer. Susie Bright is a sexually liberated bisexual who has made a name as a supporter of sexual freedom and an advisor on sex-related problems. The style is personal, the navigation easy, although the sheer volume of information presented makes reading tedious at times. On the other hand, for anybody insecure about sex or their sexuality, women in particular, this site is both useful and reassuring. The emphasis is on the US and US culture, slightly reducing its value in Britain.

overall rating:
★★★★
classification:
homepage
updated:
frequently
navigation:
★★★★★
content:
★★★★
readability:
★★★
orgasm rating:
not applicable
orgasm rating:
not applicable
speed:
★★★
US

SPECIAL FEATURES

Fourteen sections are offered, My Resumé, Susie's Shop, My Movies, Gossip, My Favorites, Rants and Raves, VIP Interviews, Why Me?, FAQs, Susie's Stories, Tour Schedule, Photo Gallery, For Writers and Sexpert Opinion. Most speak for themselves, providing information and opinions. We took a look at her resumé, which was interesting and long enough to get any biographer started. The FAQ section covers her background and ideology and we couldn't help but be impressed that she wrote pamphlets to denounce Ronald Reagan when she was eight. In Why Me? she tackles what drives her and the sexual myths and misconceptions that anger her. The emphasis is American but often true for the UK as well, and we admired her forthright style. For writers gives advice on getting erotica published and offers a discussion forum. Again, this is most valid for the US but much of her advice is more general. Susie's Stories links to stories and essays both by Susie herself and some of the authors published in The Best American Erotica. We read My First Dirty Picture which is not sexual as such but is certainly powerful for all its brevity. All in all, she comes across as strong, genuine and supportive.

OTHER FEATURES

The site also offers message boards, a chance to have Susie's newsletter emailed direct and a link to her column in Playboy Online.

A useful resource for information on sex and sexual liberation despite the American slant.

Section 12

good vibrations & other bits

The UK has seen an explosion of sex shops in recent years, and of shops specialising in sexy accessories. Rather than simply produce a national list of the biggest sex shops, we have tried to go for specialist outfits as well. All our reviews are for UK suppliers offering goods for direct sale. The list is far from comprehensive, and net shops seldom provide links to their competitors. For a longer list, www.informedconsent.co.uk provides links to most worthwhile UK outlets, although with a bias towards fetish-orientated shops. In theory, anybody with a credit card can purchase goods direct from the US and most other countries, but this is expensive and unreliable, and there are very few things not available in the UK.

Most shops use a shopping trolley system, where you can browse and shop as you go along, then make adjustments to your choice before ordering. In general ordering over the net requires credit card details, and it is wise to check that these are being transmitted over a secure link. Secure links are symbolised on the web by a shut padlock, insecure links by an open padlock.

Consumer's rights are the same with net shopping as they are with any other form of shopping. Shopping scams are relatively rare, but it is far easier to make a website vanish than a real shop, so it pays to shop with established, reputable firms. At the least, make sure than the site gives the address of their premises.

http://www.axfords.com

Axfords

This is the website for Axfords, the corsetry experts established in 1880. It is a great shopping site, if specialist, covering the full range of old-fashioned underwear in a style so deeply erotic that their catalogue has become a bible for what is perhaps the most aesthetically pleasing of fetishes. Even the company style has a pleasantly Victorian edge, presenting advice on corsetry and stressing the old-fashioned values of service, quality and confidentiality. We can personally vouch for the quality, both of workmanship and materials. The site is well laid out, fast, and easy to follow, although the sheer volume of information can slow things down. The site is designed for Netscape 4 and those using older systems may have difficulties.

SPECIAL FEATURES

The Catalogue is the heart of the site, offering an astonishing range of fabric corsets, leather corsets, knickers, bloomers, camisoles, half-slips, stockings, suspenders, wigs, and a complete maid's uniform. These are illustrated and charmingly displayed on otherwise naked models. We took a look at Corset D.11, illustrated by a girl playing croquet in her corset, stockings, and nothing else. This design is available in satin or PVC, and is lace trimmed with six suspenders attached. The price is £115, which seems like good value. We also looked at their bloomers and knickers, which are nice, but although they offer split-seam bloomers, we were disappointed not to find a full range of

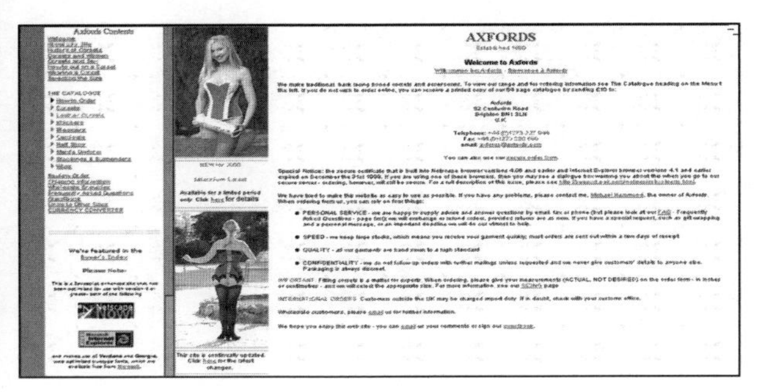

Victorian panel-back drawers. Information and advice re both provided in plenty, including not just ordering details, but also features on the History of the Corset, Corsets and Sex, Wearing a Corset, and more.

OTHER FEATURES

There are many other features, including relevant links, a guestbook, a currency converter, and the answers to frequently asked questions.

The ideal site for lovers of corsetry and all that goes with it.

overall rating:
★★★★★
classification:
shopping
updated:
frequently
navigation:
★★★★
content:
★★★★★
readability:
★★★
orgasm rating:
not applicable
orgasm rating:
not applicable
speed:
★★★★
UK

http://www.expectations.co.uk

Expectations

The site for this top leather, rubber and fetishwear store. Expectations is gay male, out, and proud, but welcoming to straight men and women as well. The range is impressive, covering mainly leatherwear, but also rubber, toys, and a little artwork. The prices are high, but then so is the quality. The site presentation is good if slightly cluttered, and fast enough. All in all, the only thing missing is the overpowering aroma of leather and body oil which hits you when you visit the shop.

SPECIAL FEATURES

Leather is the main feature of the store, with a broad range of classic, leather men's gear, from harnesses to full outfits. The quality is good, in heavy duty leather with equally heavy duty fittings. This is great stuff for presenting a powerful male erotic image, gay or otherwise.

Rubber Again, this is a good range of outfits, if less extensive. The quality is good, the range running from simple things for showing off in, right up to hoods and enclosure suits for the serious fetishist.

Other Products This is a large section split into areas for butt plugs, dildos, cock toys, nipple gear, 'medical' accessories, body jewellery, and others. As always, the quality is high. Some of the products are very definitely not for the uninitiated.

Tom of Finland Artwork is offered from this exceptional gay artist, featuring heavily-muscled and spectacularly endowed men in a range of classic and uninhibited situations.

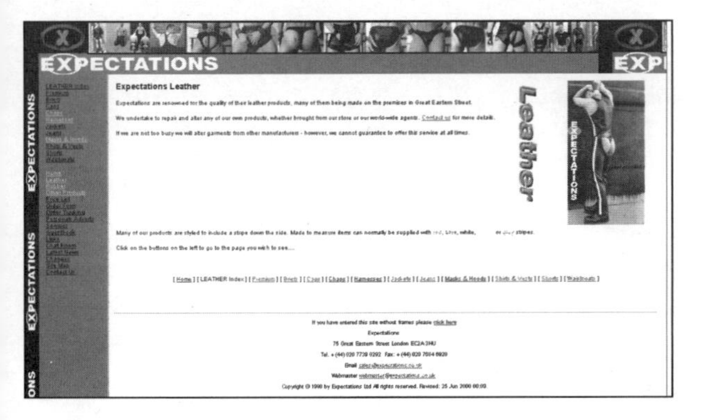

OTHER FEATURES

The site is also a good gay male resource, focussed on fetishists and offering personals, links, news, a chatroom, and more.

Top supplier for male fetish gear and toys.

overall rating:
★★★★★
classification:
shopping
updated:
frequently
navigation:
★★★★
content:
★★★★★
readability:
★★★★
orgasm rating:
♀♀♀♀
orgasm rating:
♂♂♂♂
speed:
★★★★
UK

http://www.house-of-harlot.com

House of Harlot

House of Harlot is the outstanding outfitter's for sexy rubberwear. Their range derives from the skill and imagination of the founder, Robin Archer, who blends the exotic with the erotic to create garments of wonderful originality and style. These are largely for women, but new ranges for men are planned. Quality is high, as is the price, but you get what you pay for. A range of leatherwear is also soon to be introduced, which doubtless will be as great as the rubber. The site is artistically presented and navigation is straightforward, while sales are made over a Secure Server Connection.

SPECIAL FEATURES

Online Shopping is the main feature of the site, offering thumbnailed pictures of models wearing clothes from their range. Click on these and a larger picture will appear, along with ordering details. (Anyone into rubber will love these pictures anyway, which is why we gave the site an orgasm rating). We liked the rubber City Slicker Suit, a beautiful lady's three-piece available in black, white, red or pinstripe. So cute, so cool, and just one item in an impressive range.

Galleries is a feature showing some of their past designs, from little rubber sailor suits to half-woman/half-insect outfits.

Custom Design If you want something truly unique, or just have to express an unusual costume fetish to perfection, the House of

Harlot will design and create it for you. Full rubber platemail, perhaps? No problem.

OTHER FEATURES

Stockists, relevant links, and other information are also included. The crew at House of Harlot are genuine fetishists, and their lifestyle and history also feature.

For erotic rubberwear, the best.

http://www.sh-womenstore.com

Sh!

Sh! Is the UK's first sex shop run by women and for women. Set up in 1992 as an alternative to the sleazy, over-priced Soho shops, Sh! Does not actually ban men, but only allows men to enter in the company of a woman. Although popular with lesbians, Sh! is by no means exclusively a lesbian shop, catering for women and couples of nearly all tastes. Much of the range is made by Sh!, using higher quality materials than most sex shops. Not everything available from the shop is listed on the site. Like the shop, the style of the site is definitely feminine. The design is good, and is presented in frames with a large if not entirely clear jumpstation for easy navigation. The readability suffers as many of the product pictures are too small, but otherwise this is an excellent site for an excellent shop.

SPECIAL FEATURES

Sh! stocks a broad product range, which is listed in categories on the jumpstation: playthings, buzz words, silicone dildos, harnesses, lube baby, edibles, latex love, rumpy pumpy, bound to please, nipples, pleasures, toys for two, and pc. We looked at several categories:

Toys for Two covers double ended and strap-on dildos, and clitoral stimulators for wearing on the penis. Click on each picture to go to the price list and description. Double dildos started at £22, while moulded rubber strap-ons were £75. These may sound like purely lesbian toys, but one third of all strap-on dildos sell to heterosexual couples.

Harnesses shows one of the strengths of the shop. Ten different designs of dildo harness are offered, including ones that leave the wearer's bottom accessible, and a clever design that fits on to the upper thigh.

Nipples covers a range of nipple clamps, from £12 to £40 for the vibrating version.

Bound to Please covers restraints and other bondage equipment, although the site does not list the shop's more exotic stock, such as pony-girl bridles and reins.

Pc has nothing to do with political correctness, but covers toys for pelvic floor control and exercise.

Sex Tips is a useful section giving advice on women's sexual pleasure and safe sex.

OTHER FEATURES

The site has an efficient shopping system and Sh! can be contacted direct.

The site for the UK's premier women's sex shop.

overall rating:
★★★★★
classification:
shopping
updated:
frequently
navigation:
★★★★★
content:
★★★★★
readability:
★★★★
orgasm rating:
not applicable
orgasm rating:
not applicable
speed:
★★★
UK

http://wildcat.co.uk

Wildcat

Wildcat is the UK's leading supplier of body jewellery, providing not only a truly impressive range, but an expert back-up service also. Their site reflects this, with page after page of their products beautifully illustrated in colour. The site design is excellent, both artistic and functional, with a framed jumpstation for easy navigation, and no distractions at all. Those who are new to body jewellery may occasionally be confused by the sheer variety of products and unfamiliar names; bewildered even. We did feel some of the information could have been presented more clearly, while the scale of each item was not always obvious in the photographs.

SPECIAL FEATURES

Customer Services features online information pages covering the care of piercings, jewellery advice, and shop and ordering details.

Jewellery Advice is provided and has been organised into body areas, with specific advice and recommendations given for different piercings such as ears, nostrils, and navels. The advice is extensive, but assumes a basic knowledge of piercings, while for less common piercings they advise consulting a professional piercer, including all genital piercings.

Product Ranges is the heart of the site, with Wildcat products divided into 10 categories: Mammoth Ivory, Trojan Horse, Zircon

Gold, Body Spirals, Titanium, Silver, Lavabells, Blackline, Satellites and Orbitals. The majority of these are specific styles registered by Wildcat. We looked at Lavabells, which are navel ornaments made of surgical steel and decorated with a coloured glass insert. These retail at £8, or £9 for the larger Mega Lavabell. The insert is formed from molten galls, making each one unique. When we visited, 48 were displayed, each with a reference for ease of ordering. Their Orbitals are also navel ornaments, but come in nine highly individual designs, from beautifully made silver flowers to the exotic Insectoids, and retail at around £10. The Trojan Horse range covers eight spiral designs, made from hollow surgical steel to save weight. Each design has different tips, from plain balls to exotic spiked forms. These are for large ear piercings and retail at between £40 and £60.

OTHER FEATURES

Wildcat also provides links, a guestbook, and details for ordering. Catalogues may be ordered from the site.

The UK's leading site for body jewellery.

overall rating:
★★★★
classification:
shopping
updated:
frequently
navigation:
★★★
content:
★★★★
readability:
★★★★
orgasm rating:
not applicable
orgasm rating:
not applicable
speed:
★★★
UK

http://www.annsummers.com

Ann Summers

As the UK's leading high-street chain of sex shops, Ann Summers merits an inclusion. For many, Ann Summers is the entry point to the world of sexy clothes and sex toys, mainly because they manage to be sexy without being sleazy. The site comes across in the same way; fun verging on the giggly. The structure of the site is very slick and sexy, though attempting to navigate quickly was irritating, and the pages were slow to load, although the shopping system is clear and straightforward. The site works best if you browser is Java enabled.

SPECIAL FEATURES

The entrance is a virtual lift complete with virtual bell-girl. The lift

buttons give eight choices to click on:

On-line Shopping is the heart of the sight and much the largest section. This lists the products for sale, separated into body accessories, books, condoms, fun novelties, glamour with attitude, hosiery, lingerie, men's underwear, oils and lotions, sex toys and t-shirts. Glamour with attitude proved to be sexy party outfits. Overall, the selection is large, straightfoward, and primarily designed for the female half of straight couples.

Book a Party gives you a chance to book an Ann Summers Party, where one of their agents will come to show you and your friends their products.

Virtual Postcards offers a choice of three virtual postcards to send to your friends. These are free and show pictures of models in Ann Summers lingerie.

OTHER FEATURES

4, 5, 6, 7, and 8 offer, respectively, a game, a free catalogue, the locations of their stores, a silly willy screensaver and franchise opportunities.

A big, brassy site for a big, brassy store.

overall rating:
★★★★
classification:
shopping
updated:
occasionally
navigation:
★★★★
content:
★★★★
readability:
★★★★
orgasm rating:
not applicable
orgasm rating:
not applicable
speed:
★★★★
UK

http://www.dspace.dial.pipex.com/town/way/gis93

Hide and Sleek

Hide and Sleek is a shop based in Fife, which caters almost exclusively for transvestites, where Lorraine, a real girl, provides a friendly and uncritical service. The site is their online shopping service, and offers a wide range of clothes and accessories. The site is straightforward, well presented, and easy to follow.

SPECIAL FEATURES

The Shop gives details of the outlet, which is fine if you live within reasonable distance of Fife.

Catalogue is the heart of the site, listing their stock in seventeen sub-categories: Skirts, Tops, PVC Wear, Fun Stuff, Cocktail Wear, Gloves, Bridal Wear, Lingerie, Corsets, Tights and Stockings, Wigs, Make-up, Boobs (choose from basic, push-up, or teardrop), Hip Shapers, Footwear, Jewellery, and Magazines. We took a look at fun stuff, which included four styles: maid, nurse, little girl, and school girl. These are available in various sizes and colours, and cost £30 to £160. These looked smart and seemed as suitable for forced-to-femme games or real girls as for serious transvestitism. Cocktail Wear showed a range of five frocks, including taffeta and crushed velvet, with prices from £30 to £125.

Your Designs is the made-to-measure page, offering to make up anything customers dream up. Designs can be discussed and developed, allowing you to get the best from Lorraine's

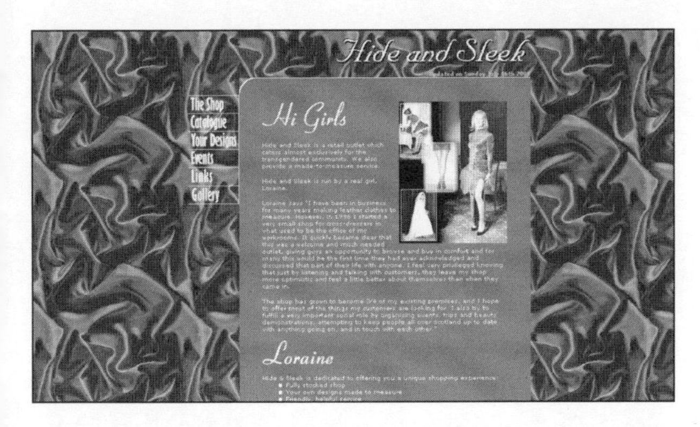

expertise to produce a perfectly-fitting finished product to suit personal preferences.

Events or at least events based in Scotland, lists the Hide and Sleek TV Beauty Exhibition, Miss TV Scotland, and support groups in Edinburgh, Glasgow, Aberdeen and Inverness.

OTHER FEATURES

Links, a sizing service and an order form are also offered.

Online frock shop especially for transvestites.

overall rating:
★★★★
classification:
shopping
updated:
frequently
navigation:
★★★★
content:
★★★★
readability:
★★★★★
orgasm rating:
not applicable
orgasm rating:
not applicable
speed:
★★★★
UK

http://www.theloveshack.co.uk

The Loveshack

The site for a large, conventional sex shop, catering for all but the most distinctive of tastes. The Loveshack is an Exeter-based sex shop offering an impressive range of products. Okay, so you can't buy a rubber piggy-girl snout or even a cane, but we liked it anyway. The style of the sight is light and playful, but without being silly, making it welcoming to all. As always with such shops, the focus is on sexy gear for women, but men are also catered for. We found navigation easy and fast, if not especially so, with clearly set out links, and an efficient shopping system. Shopping is secure.

SPECIAL FEATURES

Footwear is the Loveshack's speciality, and we were impressed by the range available from the Magic Shoe Company. It would be a fussy boot or shoe lover indeed who could not find what they wanted here. Court shoes and others are offered, along with ankle, knee, and thigh length boots. These come in leather, patent leather, suede, rubber, glitter material, and more, with red, black and white alongside more exotic colours. Glittery purple knee boots anyone? They're here. We had a look at the thigh boots, of which nine styles are offered. We liked the MS056P, which is a classic high-heeled, back-lacing thigh boot. This came in size 4 to 11, including men's sizes, and could be had in either leather or PVC for £165.

Fashions Four fashion houses are listed here, with more promised. We found some of these a bit too tame to really belong in a sex shop, but others were great, from tiny briefs to catsuits, although there was nothing really exotic. We liked the range of PVC mini-shorts from Arena.

Toys covers sex dolls, vibrators, novelties, outfits, bondage and S&M. The ranges are good for a non-specialist, including some nice, if plain rubberwear, and some basic kit for BDSM play. We took a look at the vibrators, of which 22 models are offered at reasonable prices, including doubles, strap-ons, and the famous rabbit.

OTHER FEATURES

Loveshack also offers an exchange service, wholesale terms, a currency converter, a message board, and chat.

A good sex shop site, especially for shoe and boot lovers.

overall rating:
★★★★
classification:
shopping
updated:
frequently
navigation:
★★★★
content:
★★★★
readability:
★★★
orgasm rating:
not applicable
orgasm rating:
not applicable
speed:
★★★★
UK

http://www.nicennaughty.co.uk

Nice 'n' Naughty

Nice 'n' Naughty is a Chester-based shop of which this site is the online branch. It is very much a general sex shop, with a broad range of products catering for all but the most specialist of tastes. The range is hard to fault, and is claimed to be wider still, although it is not always the best value, and the emphasis is firmly on women dressing up to look sexy. The style of the site is risqué, with an S&M touch as their in-shop dungeon is advertised. The site is fast enough and fairly easy to use, although cluttered in places.

SPECIAL FEATURES

Catalogue is an extensive range of sex products divided into lingerie, leather, latex, PVC, restraints, boots and shoes, club gear, marital aids and toys, videos, and magazines. We took a look at the Club Gear to find a large range of sexy clothing and accessories such as gloves and blindfolds. The clothes were entirely for women, and only a few were thumbnailed which is a disadvantage. Some outfits could be worn to an ordinary club, others only to a fetish or swingers' event. All in all we felt their range to be imaginative though not especially so. The lingerie range was bigger, with over 80 items, and nearly all of them thumbnailed. Some of these were very sexy indeed and we were pleased that some voluptuous girls had been included among the models. We particularly liked their range of bodystockings. The prices seem very fair. With the restraints, we finally found something for men: a ball gag! We found the range of videos and magazines impressive for a UK shop, with over 100 video titles and plenty of magazines, from plain old porn to such specialist titles as Footsie and Splosh.

Dungeon This showcases their range of BDSM-oriented gear, which we felt was very much a beginner's choice.

OTHER FEATURES

Nice 'n' Naughty may be contacted, but this is essentially a simple shopping site.

A good general shopping site with a slant towards BDSM.

overall rating:
★★★★
classification:
shopping
updated:
frequently
navigation:
★★★★
content:
★★★★
readability:
★★★
orgasm rating:
not applicable
orgasm rating:
not applicable
speed:
★★★★
UK

http://www.quality-control.co.uk

Quality Control

Quality Control are specialist suppliers of instruments for erotic discipline. Within their areas they are undoubtedly the best and are proportionally expensive. The site is clear, simple and unambiguous; easy links take you to what you want to see or order. All those products intended for erotic punishment are graded according to severity, from very gentle to very severe. The style of the site is matter-of-fact, detached even. You might think they were selling groceries, not whips and canes. We would have liked a few more pretty pictures for a five star rating.

Warning: Some of these products are potentially dangerous and should only be used by careful, sober, experienced people, preferably after a period of training from somebody with experience. And, if you are going to whip somebody, you should first know how it feels yourself. Be safe, sane, and consensual.

SPECIAL FEATURES

The sites are divided into 13 sections: whips, crops, dressage and carriage whips, show canes, traditional canes, paddles, tawses, straps, bondage and suspension, strap dress, masks, furniture, and accessories. Many of these are handmade by Quality Control. We looked at the tawses, the traditional Scots instrument of punishment. Quality Control tawses are reproduced in high-quality saddlery leather and finished to a high standard. Our favourites were the Lochgelly Tawses, made

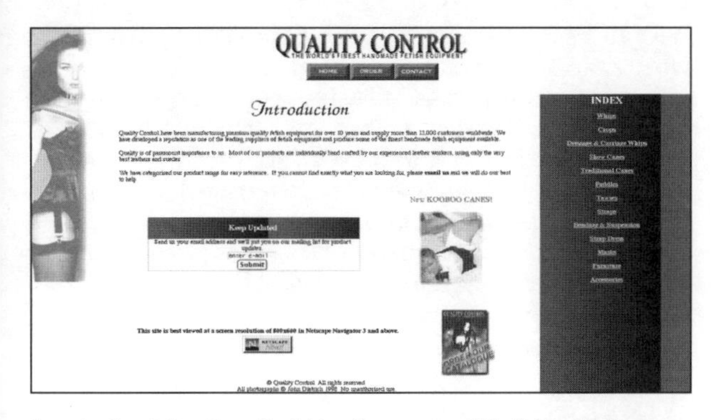

from leather taken from the hide of a 30 year-old bull. The leather was originally ordered by John J. Dick of Lochgelly, Scotland's most famous tawse-maker, but forgotten, remaining in storage until discovered by Quality Control's whip-maker. The range of whips is impressive, but the canes are koodoo, which is less good than the heavier dragon. The range of accessories really illustrates their dedication to quality, including silver- and gold-plated body jewellery.

OTHER FEATURES

The Quality Control catalogue can be ordered from the site.

The best for instruments of erotic discipline.

overall rating:
★★★★
classification:
shopping
updated:
occasionally
navigation:
★★★★
content:
★★★★
readability:
★★★★
orgasm rating:
not applicable
orgasm rating:
not applicable
speed:
★★★
UK

http://www.whatkatiedid.com

What Katie Did

This site is specialist to the point of obsession, which we loved. What Katie Did specialises in sexy, old-fashioned hosiery, especially seamed and fully-fashioned stockings. The navigation system is fine, but the site is a little slow, and we did feel the design could have been better, and sexier, but the range of stock should keep the most determined of stocking enthusiasts happy. This is a small, personal, and highly specialised shopping site, but what it lacks in size is more than made up for in enthusiasm and quality.

SPECIAL FEATURES

What Katie Did break their stock down into six areas:

Seamed Nylons This section starts with the wonderful remark that, "no woman's outfit is complete without classic seamed nylon stockings", which we felt really summed up the dedication of the site. The stockings are offered in three distinct styles: classic non-stretch nylons from Jonathon Aston, stretch nylons from Pamela Mann, and sheer champagne hose with seams in contrasting colours. So as not to be completely old-fashioned, Aristoc lace-top hold-up stockings are also offered. Full details of each product, including thumbnailed pictures, can be viewed by clicking on the Description and Products buttons.

Fully Fashioned stockings are for many the ultimate expression of the hosier's art. Sadly, they are almost extinct, but the British firm Eleganti still make a design, which What Katie Did stock. These are shaped to fit the leg, with the seam as part of the construction and not just decoration. They are exquisite, and we felt that this is the sort of rare and fine product erotic clothing shops ought to be stocking.

Vintage Stockings is a collection of original, fully-fashioned stockings made in the US. These are presented in their original boxes at what are pretty fair prices. Being collectors' items, they are available only to those on the What Katie Did mailing list or shop customers. Fully-fashioned seconds with minor defects are also offered in this section.

Fishnets, Fashion Tights and Bodywear offer a good range of cute, modern-style hosiery for those who are rather less fanatic about their legwear. More designs to come.

OTHER FEATURES

Site news and details on how to order are also available. The site is full of hints on the care and wearing of stockings.

A great little site for the serious stocking enthusiast.

http://www.x-sensual.co.uk

X-sensual worldwide

overall rating:
★★★★
classification:
shopping
updated:
occasionally
navigation:
★★★★
content:
★★★★
readability:
★★★★
orgasm rating:
not applicable
orgasm rating:
not applicable
speed:
★★★
UK

The site of a good general sex shop. X-sensual is based in Nottingham, but is intended as an international online sex shop. The range is broad, with no particular speciality but something for just about everyone. The style is polite and friendly, with recommendations for Cyber Patrol and Net Nanny. We found the site simple, fast, straightforward, and easy to use, with few distracting features. If anything, there is too little information.

SPECIAL FEATURES

Magazines are broken down into Fetish, UK Hardcore, and Contacts. We thought the range was rather small, and were disappointed to see the fetish range limited to female domination and rubber.

Novelties covers sex toys, of which there are plenty, mainly vibrators, dildos, and dolls. Fancy a rubber policewoman? She's here, for whatever purpose. We took a look at the Fist, a dildo in the shape of an upper arm, moulded in detail and presumably life-sized. This cost £24.

Clothing is much the largest section, with the emphasis firmly on sexy outfits for women. These include corsets, dresses, tops, skirts, shorts, trousers, shirts, underwear, and lingerie. Accessories, PVC items, restraints, cuffs, and masks are also included. We had a look at the corsets and bustiers, of which no less than 24 designs were offered. Our favourite was the

Fully-Boned Thong Basque. This was offered in sizes eight to 24, which impressed us, and in a choice of rubber, leather, or gloss PVC. All materials come in black, with rubber and PVC in a few other colours.

OTHER FEATURES

A currency converter and ordering advice are included.

A good, general online sex store.

overall rating:
★★★
classification:
shopping
updated:
variably
navigation:
★★
content:
★★★★★
readability:
★★★★★
orgasm rating:
not applicable
orgasm rating:
not applicable
speed:
★★★★
UK

http://www.amazon.co.uk

Amazon.co.uk

While not technically an erotic site, Amazon.co.uk probably offers a wider range of erotic literature than any other online bookstore. Unfortunately, they are remarkably coy about this, and we had great difficulty in accessing their selection. Technically, erotica comes under the Literature and Fiction category, but their browse facility does not include it as a topic, while many well-known erotic authors are not included in their author lists. This attitude struck us as more appropriate to the 1950s than the year 2000, and we only managed to find what we wanted because we knew some authors' names and could feed them into the general search facility. Once we had found one book, links were provided to similar books, although these often led us in circles. Other than this problem, the site is fast, well designed, and easy to follow. In the end they proved to stock every erotic title we could think of in print, and a great many others, hence the five stars for content.

SPECIAL FEATURES

Amazon's range is enormous, so we chose to look at some of the better-known authors of modern erotica. We started with Aishling Morgan's Devon Cream, which is quite highly ranked and has earned four stars in the Amazon review ratings. The story is set at the beginning of the century and follows the innocent and wilful Octavia Challacombe as she is gradually corrupted. This sounds tame enough until you discover that the sex involves spanking, bondage, and a sort of human dairy. Tame it is not. The author's other books, all equally weird and wonderful, were easily found, along with links to others, mainly from the Nexus imprint. Yolanda Celbridge, Maria del Rey, Penny Birch, and Lindsay Gordon were all there. Erotica aimed specifically at women and written only by women was easier to find, with the Black Lace imprint included under adult romance. Why this should be when the content of Black Lace can be every bit as strong as that of Nexus, we do not know.

OTHER FEATURES

Amazon has an impressive range of features, including opportunities for reader reviews, comments by authors and editors, and a ranking system.

A great online store for literary erotica, if you can find it!

glossary

A

Accelerators Add-on programs, which speed up browsing.

Acceptable Use Policy These are the terms and conditions of using the internet. They are usually set by organisations, who wish to regulate an individual's use of the internet. For example, an employer might issue a ruling on the type of email which can be sent from an office.

Access Provider A company which provides access to the internet, usually via a dial-up account. Many companies such as AOL and Dircon charge for this service, although there are an increasing number of free services such as Freeserve, Lineone and Tesco.net. Also known as an Internet Service Provider.

Account A user's internet connection, with an Access/ Internet Service Provider, which usually has to be paid for.

Acrobat Reader Small freely-available program, or web browser plug-in, which lets you view a Portable Document Format (PDF) file.

Across Lite Plug-in which allows you to complete crossword puzzles online.

Address Location name for email or internet site, which is the online equivalent of a postal address. It is usually composed of a unique series of words and punctuation, such as *my.name@myhouse.co.uk*. See also URL.

America Online (AOL) World's most heavily subscribed online service provider.

Animated GIF Low-grade animation technique used on websites.

ASCII Stands for American Standard Code for Information Interchange, It is a coding standard which all computers can recognise, and ensures that if a character is entered on one part of the internet, the same character will be seen elsewhere.

ASCII Art Art made of letters and other symbols. Because it is made up of simple text, it can be recognised by different computers.

ASDL Stands for Asynchronous Digital Subscriber Line, which is a high speed copper wire which will allow rapid transfer of information. Not widely in use at moment, though the government is pushing for its early introduction.

Attachment A file included with an email, which may be composed of text, graphics and sound. Attachments are encoded for transfer across the internet, and can be viewed in their original form by the recipient. An attachment is the equivalent of putting a photograph with a letter in the post.

B

Bookmark A function of the Netscape Netvigator browser which allows you to save a link to your favourite web pages, so that you can return straight there at a later date, without having to re-enter the address. Favourites in internet Explorer is the same thing.

BPS Abbreviation of Bits Per Second, which is a measure of the speed at which information is transferred or downloaded.

Browse Common term for looking around the web. See also Surfing.

Browser A generic term for the software that allows users to move and look around the Web. Netscape Navigator and Internet Explorer are the ones that most people are familiar with, and they account for 97 percent of web hits.

Bulletin Board Service A BBS is a computer with a telephone connection, which allows you direct contact to upload and download information and converse with other users, via the computer. It was the forerunner to the online services and virtual communities of today.

C

Cache A temporary storage space on the hard drive of your computer, which stores downloaded websites. When you return to a website, information is retrieved from the cache and displayed much more rapidly. However, this information may not be the most recent version for sites which are frequently updated and you will need to reload the Website address for these.

Chat Talking to other users on the web in real time, but with typed, instead of spoken words. Special software such as ICQ or MIRC is required before you can chat.

Chat Room An internet channel which allows several people to type in their messages, and talk to one another over the internet.

Clickstream The trail left as you 'click' your way around the web.

Content The material on a website that actually relates to the site, and is hopefully of interest or value. Things like adverts are not considered to be part of the content. The term is also used to refer to information on the internet that can be seen by users, as opposed to programming and other background information.

Cookie A cookie is a nugget of information sometimes sent by websites to your hard drive when you visit.They contain such details as what you looked at, what you ordered, and can add more information, so that the website can be customized to suit you.

Cybercafe Cafe where you can use a computer terminal to browse the net for a small fee.

Cyberspace When first coined by the sci-fi author William Gibson, it meant a shared hallucination which occured when people logged on to computer networks. Now, it refers to the virtual space you're in when on the internet.

D

Dial Up A temporary telephone connection to your ISP's computer and how you make contact with your ISP, each time you log onto the Internet.

Domain The part of an Internet address which identifies an individual computer, and can often be a business or person's name. For example, in the goodwebguide.com the domain name is theGoodWebGuide.

Download Transfer of information from an Internet server to your computer.

Dynamic HTML The most recent version of the HTML standard.

E

Ecash Electronic cash, used to make transactions on the internet.

Ecommerce The name for business which is carried out over the internet.

Email Mail which is delivered electronically over the internet, usually comprised of text, but can contain illustrations, music and animations. Mail is sent to an email address, which is the internet equivalent of a postal address.

Encryption A process whereby information is scrambled to produce a 'coded message', so that it can't be read whilst in transit on the internet. The recipient must have decryption software in order to read the message.

Expire Term referring to newsgroup postings which are automatically deleted after a fixed period of time.

Ezine Publication on the web, which is updated regularly.

F

FAQ Stands for frequently asked questions and is a common section on websites where the most common enquiries and their answers are archived.

Frame A method which splits web pages into several windows.

FTP/File Transfer Protocol Standard method for transporting files across the internet.

G

GIF/Graphics Interchange Format A format in which graphics are compressed, and a popular method of putting images onto the internet, as they take little time to download.

Gopher The gopher was the precursor of the world wide web and consisted of archives accessed through a menu, usually organised by subject.

GUI/Graphical User Interface. This is the system which turns binary information into the words and images format you can see on your computer screen. For example, instead of seeing the computer language which denotes the presence of your toolbar, you actually see a toolbar.

H

Hackers A term used to refer to expert programmers who used their skills to break into computer systems, just for the fun of it. Nowadays the word is more commonly associated with computer criminals, or Crackers.

Header Basic indication of what's in an email: who it's from, when it was sent, and what it's about.

Hit When a file is downloaded from a website it is referred to as a 'hit'. Measuring the number of hits is a rough method of counting how many people visit a website. Except that it's not wholly accurate as one website can contain many files, so one visit by an individual may generate several hits.

Homepage Most usually associated with a personal site, produced by an individual, but can also refer to the first page on your browser, or the first page of a website.

Host Computer on which a website is stored. A host computer may store several websites, and usually has a fast powerful connection to the internet. Also known as a Server.

HTML/Hypertext Mark-Up Language The computer code used to construct web pages.

HTTP/Hypertext Transfer Protocol The protocol for moving HTML files across the web.

Hyperlink A word or graphic formatted so that when you click on it, you move from one area to another. See also hypertext.

Hypertext Text within a document which is formatted so it acts as a link from one page to another, or from one document to another.

I

Image Map A graphic which contains hyperlinks.

Interface What you actually see on the computer screen.

Internet One or more computers connected to one another is an internet (lower case i). The Internet is the biggest of all the internets. and consists of a worldwide collection of interconnected computer networks.

Internet Explorer One of the most popular pieces of browser software, produced by Microsoft.

Intranet A network of computers, which works in the same way as an internet, but for internal use, such as within a corporation.

ISDN/Integrated Services Digital Network Digital telephone line which facilitates very fast connections and can transfer larges amounts of data. It can carry more than one form of data at once.

ISP/Internet Service Provider See Access Provider.

J

Java Programming language which can be used to create interactive multimedia effects on webpages. The language is used to create programmes known as *applets* that add features such as animations, sound and even games to websites.

Javascript A scripting language which, like Java, can be used to add extra multimedia features. However, in contrast with Java it does not consist of separate programmes. Javascript is embedded into the HTML text and can interpreted by the browser, provided that the user has a javascript enabled browser.

JPEG Stands for 'Joint Photographic Experts Group' and is the name given to a type of format which compresses photos, so that they can be seen on the web.

K

Kill file A function which allows a user to block incoming information from unwanted sources. Normally used on email and newsreaders.

L

LAN/Local Area Network A type of internet, but limited to a single area, such as an office.

Login The account name or password needed to access a computer system.

Link Connection between web pages, or one web document and another, which are accessed via formatted text and graphic.

M

Mailing List A discussion group which is associated with a website. Participants send their emails to the site, and it is copied and sent by the server to other individuals on the mailing list.

Modem A device for converting digital data into analogue signals for transmission along standard phone lines. The usual way for home users to connect to the internet or log into their email accounts. May be internal (built into the computer) or external (a desk-top box connected to the computer).

MP3 A compressed music file format, which has almost no loss of quality although the compression rate may be very high.

N

Netscape Popular browser, now owned by AOL.

Newbie Term for someone new to the Internet. Used perjoratively of newcomers to bulletin boards or chat, who commit the sin of asking obvious questions or failing to observe the netiquette.

Newsgroup Discussion group amongst Internet users who share a mutual interest. There are thousands of newsgroups covering every possible subject.

O

Offline Not connected to the internet via a telephone line.

Online Connected to the internet via a telephone line.

Offline Browsing A function of the browser software, which allows the user to download pages and read them whilst offline.

Online Service Provider Similar to an access provider, but provides addtional features such as live chat.

P

PDF/Portable Document Format A file format created by Adobe for offline reading of brochures, reports and other documents with complex graphic design, which can be read by anyone with Acrobat Reader.

Plug-in Piece of software which adds more functions (such as playing music or video) to another, larger software program.

POP3/Post Office Protocol An email protocol that allows you to pick up your mail from any location on the web.

Portal A website which offers many services, such as search engines, email and chat rooms, and to which people are likely to return to often . ISPs such as Yahoo and Alta Vista provide portal sites which are the first thing you see when you log on, and in theory act as gateways to the rest of the web.

Post/Posting Information sent to a usenet group, bulletin board, message board or by email.

PPP/Point to Point Protocol The agreed way of sending data over dial-up connections, so that the user's computer, the modem and the Internet Server can all recognise it. It is the protocol which allows you to get online.

Protocol Convention detailing a set of actions that computers in a network must follow so that they can understand one another.

Q

Query Request for specific information from a database.

R

RAM /Random Access Memory Your computer's short term memory.

Realplayer G2 A plug-in program that allows you to view video in real-time and listen to sound and which is becoming increasingly important for web use.

Router A computer program which acts as an interface between two networks, and decides how to route information.

S

Searchable Database A database on a website which allows the user to search for information, usually be keyword.

Search Engine Programs which enable web users to search for pages and sites using keywords. They are usually to be found on portal sites and browser homepages. Infoseek, Alta Vista and Lycos are some of the popular search engines.

Secure Transactions Information transfers which are encrypted so that only the sender and recipient have access to the uncoded message, so that the details within remain private. The term is most commonly used to refer to credit card transactions, although other information can be sent in a secure form.

Server A powerful computer that has a permanent fast connection to the internet. Such computers are usually owned by companies and act as host computers for websites.

Sign-on To connect to the internet and start using one of its facilities.

Shareware Software that doesn't have to be paid for or test version of software that the user can access for free, as a trial before buying it.

Standard A style which the whole of the computer industry has agreed upon. Industry standards mean that hardware and software produced by the various different computer companies will work with one another.

Surfing Slang for looking around the Internet, without any particular aim, following links from site to site.

T

TLA/Three Letter Acronyms Netspeak for the abbreviations of net jargon, such as BPS (Bits Per Second) and ISP (Internet Service Provider).

U

Upload To send files from your computer to another one on the internet. When you send an email you are uploading a file.

URL/Uniform Resource Locator Jargon for an address on the internet, such as www.thegoodwebguide.co.uk.

Usenet A network of newsgroups, which form a worldwide system, on which anyone can post 'news'.

V

Virtual Community Name given to a congregation of regular mailing list/ newsgroup users.

VRML/Virtual Reality Modeling Language Method for creating 3D environments on the web.

W

Wallpaper Description of the sometimes hectic background patterns which appear behind the text on some websites.

Web Based Email/Webmail Email accounts such as Hotmail and Rocketmail, which are accessed via an Internet browser, rather than an email program such as Outlook Express. Webmail has to be typed whilst the user is online, but can accessed from anywhere on the Web.

Webmaster A person responsible for a web server. May also be known as System Administrator.

Web Page Document which forms one part of a website (though some sites are a single page), usually formatted in HTML.

Web Ring Loose association of websites which are usually dedicated to the same subject and often contain links to one another.

Website A collection of related web pages which often belong to an individual or organisation and are about the same subject.

World Wide Web The part of the Internet which is easy to get around and see.The term is often mistakely interchanged with Internet, though the two are not the same. If the Internet is a shopping mall, with shops, depots, and delivery bays, then the web is the actual shops which the customers see and use.

index

Great titles in thegoodwebguide series:

paperback £4.99

games

ISBN 1-903282-10-1

music

ISBN 1-903282-11-X

sex

ISBN 1-903282-09-8

hardback £12.99

food	ISBN 1-903282-01-2
gardening	ISBN 1-903282-00-4
genealogy	ISBN 1-903282-06-3
health	ISBN 1-903282-08-X
money	ISBN 1-903282-02-0
parents	ISBN 1-903282-03-9
travel	ISBN 1-903282-05-5
wine	ISBN 1-903282-04-7